CAKE DECORATING
ESSENTIAL SKILLS AND TECHNIQUES

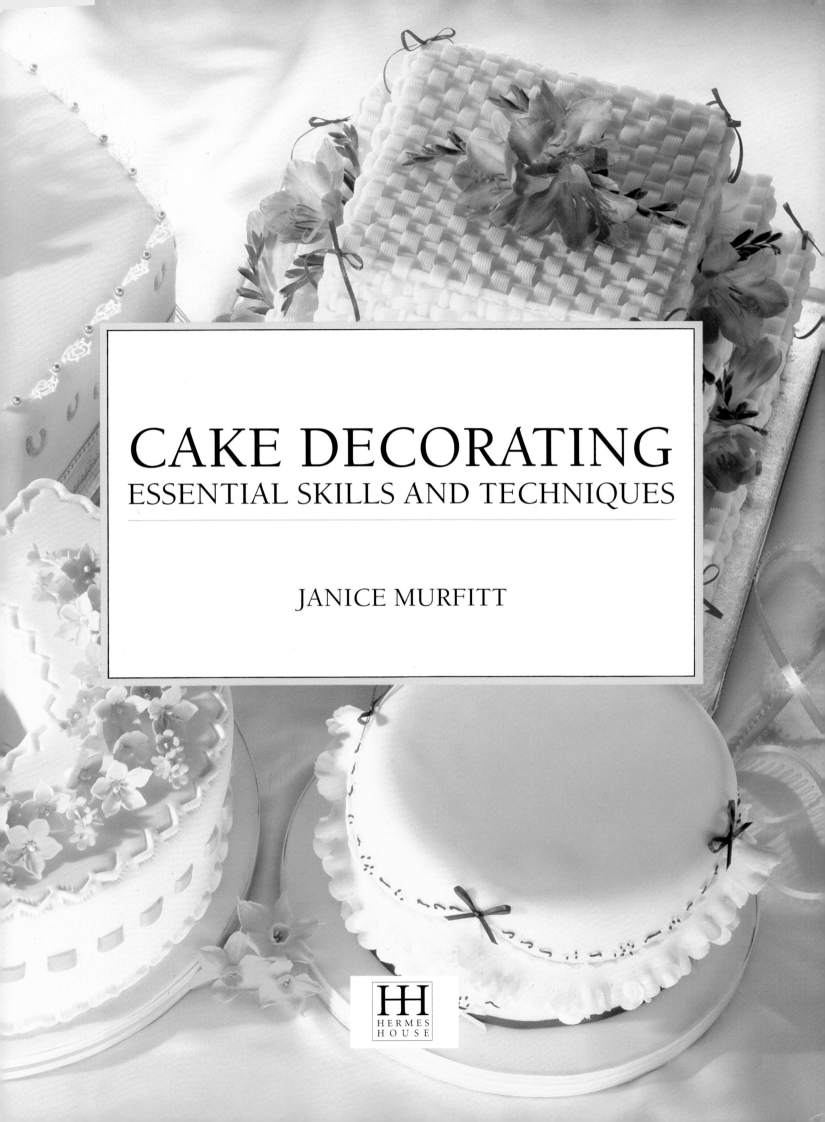

CAKE DECORATING
ESSENTIAL SKILLS AND TECHNIQUES

JANICE MURFITT

HERMES
HOUSE

This edition published by Hermes House

© Anness Publishing Limited 2002

Hermes House is an imprint of Anness Publishing Limited
Hermes House, 88–89 Blackfriars Road, London SE1 8HA

Published in the USA by Hermes House, Anness Publishing Inc.
27 West 20th Street, New York, NY 10011

Publisher: Joanna Lorenz
Project Editor: Judith Simons
Art Director: Peter Bridgewater
Designer: James Lawrence
Photographer: David Armstrong
Production Controller: Joanna King

Printed and bound in Singapore

© Anness Publishing Limited 1995, 1999,
Updated © 2002
5 7 9 10 8 6 4

Measurements

Three sets of equivalent measurements have been provided
in the recipes here, in the following order: Metric, Imperial
and American. The golden rule is never to mix units of
measure within a recipe. The conversions are approximate,
but accurate enough to ensure successful results.

CONTENTS

Baking and Decorating Techniques

INTRODUCTION

*B*AKING AND DECORATING TECHNIQUES *covers all aspects of cake making, icing and decorating and has been carefully planned to take you step by step through all the stages and methods involved. Beginning with the basics, there are tried and tested recipes for a wide variety of classic sponge and fruit cakes and simple icings and frostings for quick-and-easy baking. There are also recipes for the classic cake coverings – marzipan, sugarpaste (fondant) and royal icing – plus step-by-step guides to covering square and round cakes.*

When it comes to the final decoration on a cake, this is where your own creative skills and imagination can be used to full effect.

8

There are many techniques included here from simple bought decorations, such as coloured ribbons and flowers, and sweets (candies), nuts and crystallized fruits, to chocolate run-outs, curls and cut-outs. Marzipan and sugarpaste (fondant) can be coloured and moulded or modelled into fruit and flower shapes, used for cut-out flowers, frills and abstract decorations, and for crimped and embossed designs. Finally, royal icing, perhaps the most difficult medium to work with, can be piped to produce the daintiest lace pieces, sugar flowers, run-outs and beautiful borders. Follow the detailed illustrated step-by-step guides to perfect cake making and decorating to create a host of varied finishes, from the simple to the lavish.

BAKING TECHNIQUES

Cake-making Equipment

To obtain the very best results when making cakes, it is necessary to have a selection of good equipment. Start with the basic items that are needed immediately, then gradually add to your collection as your skills progress. Always buy good quality equipment, and with care it will not need replacing.

1 Cooling rack
2 Scissors
3 Cakeboards
4 Electric hand mixer
5 Wire whisk
6 Scales
7 Cake boxes
8 Measuring jug
9 Cutters
10 Ruler
11 Mixing bowls
12 Greaseproof (wax) paper
13 Baking parchment
14 Baking sheets
15 Pastry brushes
16 Cling film (plastic wrap)
17 Plastic spatula
18 Wooden spoon
19 Baking tins (pans)
20 Knife
21 Palette knife (spatula)
22 Cranked-handle palette knife (spatula)
23 Pencils
24 Standard measuring spoons
25 Standard measuring cups

GENERAL EQUIPMENT

The following items will be needed for making basic cakes and icings and for simple cake decorating:

SCALES – accurate scales for weighing all cake ingredients are essential. Without them, good results cannot be achieved. Choose scales with separate weights for the most accurate results.

MEASURING JUG – with metric, imperial and cup measurements for accurate measuring of liquids in millilitres, fluid ounces or pints, or dry and liquid ingredients in cup sizes.

STANDARD MEASURING SPOONS – for spoon measurements which are constantly accurate for dry and liquid ingredients; general spoons vary in size, causing inaccurate measurement.

STANDARD MEASURING CUPS – like the spoons, these give a constantly accurate measurement for dry ingredients and liquids.

WOODEN SPOONS – a selection of wooden spoons with handles of varying lengths, suitable for beating large or small quantities of mixture.

WHISKS – a small hand rotary whisk or a wire whisk are necessary for whisking cream, egg whites or light mixtures to give a smooth consistency.

ELECTRIC HAND MIXERS – invaluable for whisking mixtures over hot water, such as whisked sponge cake or cooked meringues.

ELECTRIC FOOD MIXERS – these more efficient mixers are necessary when making large quantities of cake mixtures or icings for wedding cakes or special occasions. Care must be taken when using not to over-mix.

FOOD PROCESSORS – ideal for chopping ingredients quickly, beating butter icing or for cake mixtures. Care must be taken not to over-process mixtures.

PLASTIC OR WOODEN MIXING SPATULAS – these come in many shapes and sizes, usually made with a flexible plastic blade. Essential for folding ingredients thoroughly into lightly-whipped mixtures or cake batters, and for removing all the mixture from the bowl.

BOWLS – a selection of small, medium and large heatproof bowls in glass or china, with smooth rounded insides for thorough, even mixing when using a wooden spoon or an electric mixer.

TINS (PANS) AND MOULDS – always choose the best quality tins (pans) for baking. The thickness of the metal prevents overcooking and ensures the tins (pans) retain their shape without bending or warping.

BAKING SHEETS – choose heavy-duty baking sheets with flat edges which will not warp in the oven. These are necessary for baking meringues, pastry or sponge cake layers. Baking sheets which have sides are ideal for standing cake tins (pans) on in the oven.

COOLING RACKS – obtainable in different sizes, round or oblong, with wide or narrow mesh. It is advisable to have a selection.

PAPERS – greaseproof (waxed) paper, baking parchment, run-out silk and rice papers all have their own use. Greaseproof (wax) paper is suitable for lining tins; finer waxed paper and run-out silk, if available, is flexible and ideal for icing run-outs and piped decorations; baking parchment is ideal for meringues, spreading melted chocolate, drying moulded or cut-out sugar decorations; rice paper is for biscuits, macaroons and meringue mixture.

GLAZING BRUSHES – small and medium brushes are useful for brushing tins and moulds with melted fat or oil. A larger size is required for brushing cakes with glaze.

CUTTERS – a set of plain round and fluted cutters is always useful; fancy biscuit (cookie) cutters are available in many sizes and you will find endless uses for them.

KNIVES – a selection of small, medium and large knives are necessary for preparing ingredients and for cutting cakes into layers.

METAL PALETTE KNIVES (SPATULAS) – small, medium and large straight palette knives (spatulas) with flexible blades are used for loosening cakes from tins, and for applying, spreading and smoothing icing. A small cranked-handle palette knife (spatula) is ideal for lifting and transferring small and fragile icing decorations.

RULER, SCISSORS AND PENCIL – always needed when making cakes.

CAKEBOARDS – available in many different shapes and sizes, the most popular being rounds and squares. Use thick cakeboards for large iced (frosted) cakes and wedding cakes, and the thin cakeboards for light cakes with butter or cream icing (frosting).

BOXES – cake boxes are invaluable when making celebration cakes; once they have been made and placed on a cakeboard, they can be stored in boxes to keep them clean, dry and free from damage.

Cake Tins (Pans)

It is so important to have the correct size and shaped tin (pan) for the recipe you are following in order to get the best results. If the tin (pan) size or shape is incorrect, it will not only affect the size and depth of the cake, but also the cooking time, texture and appearance.

Always measure a cake tin (pan) across the base, not the top, to give an accurate measurement.

CHOOSING CAKE TINS (PANS)

The quality of cake tins (pans) is just as important, especially for cakes that require long, slow cooking. They should always be made of the best quality metal and have a fixed base which will not distort during cooking, or bend easily during handling or storing. Good cake tins (pans) are an investment; they only need to be purchased once if they are looked after properly.

Always line cake tins (pans) with greaseproof (wax) paper whenever possible, unless the recipe states otherwise; this will prevent marking or discolouring of the tin (pan). Wash and dry the tin (pan) thoroughly and store in a warm place to prevent rusting.

HIRING CAKE TINS (PANS)

Unusual-shaped cake tins (pans) are fun to use, especially when making a celebration cake. Rather than incurring the expense of a specially-shaped tin (pan) which you may only use once, it may be better to hire one.

These tins (pans) come in a variety of shapes and sizes and are available for hire through many kitchen shops, cake-icing specialists or bakeries. They normally require a deposit for the tin (pan), then a small hire fee which is charged at a daily rate.

Lining Cake Tins (Pans)

Cake tins (pans) are lined in different ways, depending on the type of cake you are making. Sometimes tins (pans) are only lightly greased and floured, as when making a light whisked sponge cake mixture. In this way the shape holds to the sides of the tin (pan) during cooking; if paper-lined, it would pull away, producing a misshapen cake.

Most cakes, however, are baked in tins (pans) lined with greaseproof (wax) paper. Sometimes only the base is covered for a cake requiring short-term cooking. Both the base and sides are lined when cakes need longer cooking, or for richer cake mixtures which may stick to the tin (pan), causing difficulty when turning out. Swiss (jelly) roll tins (pans) have to be lined neatly with one piece of paper so the cake can be turned out of the tin (pan) quickly to form into a roll. Cakes which need long-term cooking, such as fruit cakes, require a double thickness of paper inside the tin (pan) and the protection of double thickness brown paper around the outside so that the cake cooks evenly throughout.

Generally cake tins (pans) are brushed with melted vegetable fat or oil and lined with single or double thickness greaseproof (wax) paper. Non-stick baking parchment paper, which is slightly thicker, may also be used, especially if mixtures need to be turned out quickly.

Lining a Sandwich Tin (Shallow Cake Pan)

1 Place the tin (pan) over a piece of greaseproof (wax) paper. Using a pencil, draw around the outside of the tin (pan). Cut out the shape using a pair of sharp scissors.
2 Brush the tin (pan) lightly with melted vegetable fat or oil and fit the greaseproof (wax) paper shape over the base of the tin (pan). Brush the paper with melted white fat or oil.

MIXING CAKES SUCCESSFULLY

There are a few simple guidelines which must be followed to achieve the best results when making any cake.

● Unlike many recipes, those for cakes must be followed accurately. Measure all the ingredients carefully with scales or measuring cups, spoons and a measuring jug. Do not be tempted to add a little extra of any ingredient as this will upset the balance.
● Always make sure you have the correct shape and size of tin (pan) for the recipe, otherwise this will affect the depth of the cake, the cooking time and the texture.
● Make sure the tin (pan) is properly prepared and lined for cooking the recipe you have chosen to make.
● Check that you have all the necessary ingredients that are stated in the recipe, and that they are at the right temperature.
● Eggs should be size 3, unless otherwise stated. Farm eggs impart a wonderful flavour, but unless they are graded they may be too large for cakes, making the mixture slack.
● Ensure soft margarine is kept chilled in the refrigerator to maintain the right consistency, and leave butter out to become room temperature and soft for creaming.

● Sift all dry ingredients to help aerate the mixture and to disperse lumps.
● When making cakes by hand, beat well with a wooden spoon until the mixture is light and glossy; scrape down the mixture during beating with a plastic mixing spatula to ensure even mixing.
● If a cake is being made in a food processor or an electric mixer, be very careful not to overprocess or overbeat. This will cause the mixture to collapse and dip in the middle during baking. Remember to scrape down the batter with a plastic spatula during mixing, and to follow the manufacturer's instructions for the best results.
● If ingredients have to be folded into a mixture, use a plastic spatula with a flexible blade to cut through the mixture, turning it over and at the same time moving the bowl. Do not be tempted to stir, or be heavy-handed with, the mixture or it will lose air and become heavy.
● Level mixtures in the tin (pan) before baking, to ensure the cake top is flat when baked.
● Do check that your oven is at the correct temperature before cooking the cake.
● Test the cake before the stated cooking time as this is only a guide, and test the cake again before removing it from the oven.

COOKING CAKES SUCCESSFULLY

Many problems arise when cooking cakes, mainly because ovens do vary. Factors affecting cooking results include the heat source. Some ovens are hot, others are slow, others are fan-assisted. Recipes always give cooking times, but you must remember these times are simply a guide. At the same time, the guidelines below assume the recipes and tin (pan) sizes have been followed as advised.

• Do check that your oven is preheated to the temperature stated in the recipe. Failure to do so will affect the rising of the cake and the cooking time.
• If the cake appears to be cooked before the given time, it may indicate that the oven is hot; conversely, if it takes longer to cook, it means the oven is slow.

• A good test is to cook a homemade two-egg quick mix cake in a 20 cm/8 in sandwich tin (shallow cake pan) for about 35–40 minutes at 160°C/325°F/Gas 3. The cake should appear level and lightly browned. If the cake is cooked before the time, adjust the setting lower in the future, or higher for a cake which takes longer.
• The temperature of the cake mixture can cause the cooking time to vary. If conditions are cold, the mixture will be cold and take longer to cook; in the same way, if it is warm cooking time will be slightly quicker.
• The surface of the cake should be evenly browned and level; if the cake is overcooked on one side or risen to one side, the heating of the oven is uneven or the oven shelf is not level.

Lining a Swiss (Jelly) Roll Tin

1 Place the tin (pan) in the centre of a piece of greaseproof (wax) paper, 2.5 cm/1 in larger all round than the tin (pan). Cut from the corner of the paper to the corner of the tin (pan), using a pair of sharp scissors.
2 Lightly brush the tin (pan) with melted vegetable fat or oil and fit the paper into the tin (pan), neatly pressing into the corners. Brush the paper lightly with melted vegetable fat or oil.

Lining a Deep Cake Tin (Pan)

1 Place the tin (pan) on a double thickness of greaseproof (wax) paper or baking parchment. Draw around the base with a pencil. Cut out the marked shape with a pair of scissors.
2 Cut a strip of double thickness greaseproof (wax) paper or baking parchment long enough to wrap around the outside of the tin (pan), leaving a small overlap. It should stand 2.5 cm/1 in above the top of the tin (pan).

3 Brush the base and sides of the tin (pan) with melted vegetable fat or oil. Place the double strip of paper inside the tin (pan), pressing well against the sides and making sharp creases if it must fit into corners. Place the cut-out shape in the base of the tin and press it flat.
4 Brush the base and side papers well with melted vegetable fat or oil. Place a strip of double thickness brown paper around the outside of the tin (pan) and tie securely with string.

Line a baking (cookie) sheet with three or four layers of brown paper and stand the tin (pan) on top.

Testing Cakes

• Always check the cake five or ten minutes before the given cooking time is completed, just in case the oven is a little fast. It is always better to slightly under-cook a cake, since the mixture continues to cook in the tin (pan) after removing it from the oven.

• Always test the cake immediately before removing it from the oven, just in case it is not ready at the advised time. This could be due to a slow oven.

• For all cakes – other than fruit cakes – test by pressing very lightly on the centre of the cake with the fingers; if it springs back, the cake is cooked. Otherwise your fingers will leave a slight depression, indicating the cake needs extra cooking time. Retest at five-minute intervals.

• Fruit cakes are best tested using a warmed skewer inserted into the centre of the cake. If the skewer comes out clean, the cake is ready. Otherwise return the cake to the oven and retest at ten-minute intervals.

Storing Cakes

Everyday cakes, sponges and meringues may be kept in an airtight container or simply wrapped in cling film (plastic wrap) or foil; this will ensure they keep moist and fresh with the exclusion of the air. Store the cakes in a cool, dry place for up to a week; meringues will store for up to one month. Avoid warm, moist conditions as this will encourage mould growth.

To store fruit cakes, leave the lining paper on the cakes. This seals onto the surface during cooking and keeps the cakes moist and fresh. Wrap the cakes in a double layer of foil and keep in a cool place. Never seal a fruit cake in an air-tight container for long periods of time as this may encourage mould growth.

Rich, heavy fruit cakes keep well because of their high fruit content; although they are moist and full of flavour, they are at their best when they are first made. Such cakes do mature with keeping, but most should be consumed within three months. If you are going to keep a fruit cake for several months before marzipanning or icing it, pour over alcohol a little at a time at monthly intervals, turning the cake each time.

Light fruit cakes are stored in the same way as their rich cousins, but since they have less fruit in them, their keeping qualities are not so good. These cakes are at their best when first made, or eaten within one month of making.

For longterm storage, fruit cakes are better frozen in their double wrapping and foil.

Once the cakes have been marzipanned and iced, they will keep longer. But iced cakes must be stored in cardboard boxes in a warm, dry atmosphere, to maintain them dust-free and in good condition. Damp and cold are the worst conditions, causing the icing to stain and colourings to run.

Freeze a decorated celebration cake in the cake box, ensuring the lid is sealed with tape. Take the cake out of its box and defrost it slowly in a cool, dry place. When the cake has thawed, transfer to a warm, dry place to ensure the icing dries completely. Wedding cakes which have been kept for a long time may need re-icing and decorating.

CALCULATING QUANTITIES AND CUTTING CAKES

To work out the number of servings from a round or square cake is extremely simple and the final total depends on whether you require just a small finger of cake or a more substantial slice.

Whether the cake is round or square, cut across the cake from edge to edge into about 2.5 cm/1 in slices, thinner if desired. (Do not cut a round cake into wedges.) Cut each slice into 4 cm/1½ in pieces or thereabouts.

Using these guidelines, it should be easy to calculate the number of cake slices you can cut from any given size cake. A square cake is larger than a round cake of the same proportions and will yield more slices. On a round cake the slices become smaller at the curved edges, and the first and last slice of the cake is mainly marzipan and icing. Always keep this in mind when calculating the servings.

Example
According to the measurements above a 20 cm/8 in square cake will yield about 40 slices and a 20 cm/8 in round cake will yield about 35 slices.

BASIC CAKE RECIPES

A quick mix sponge cake is light and fluffy; ideal for this springtime cake decorated with lemon butter icing and marzipan flowers.

Quick Mix Sponge Cake

This is a quick-and-easy reliable recipe for making everyday cakes in various sizes, shapes and flavours.

INGREDIENTS	2-EGG QUANTITY	3-EGG QUANTITY	4-EGG QUANTITY
• Self-raising flour	125 g/4 oz/1 cup	175 g/6 oz/1½ cups	225 g/8 oz/2 cups
• Baking powder	5 ml/1 tsp/1 tsp	7.5 ml/1½ tsp/1½ tsp	10 ml/2 tsp/2 tsp
• Caster (superfine) sugar	125 g/4 oz/½ cup	175 g/6 oz/¾ cup	225 g/8 oz/1 cup
• Soft margarine	125 g/4 oz/½ cup	175 g/6 oz/¾ cup	225 g/8 oz/1 cup
• Eggs	2	3	4

1 Preheat the oven to 170°C/325°F/Gas 3. Prepare the tin (pan) according to the recipe.

2 Sift the flour and baking powder into a bowl. Add sugar, margarine and eggs. Mix together with a wooden spoon, then beat for 1–2 minutes until smooth and glossy.

3 Stir in chosen flavourings and beat until evenly blended.

4 Pour into prepared tin (pan), level the top and bake as required.

CHOICE OF FLAVOURINGS

The following amounts are for a 2-egg quantity cake. Increase the suggested flavourings to suit the quantity being made.

Citrus – 10 ml/2 tsp/2 tsp finely grated orange, lemon or lime rind
Chocolate – add 15 ml/1 tbsp/1 tbsp cocoa blended with 15 ml/1 tbsp/1 tbsp boiling water, or 25 g/1 oz/scant ¼ cup chocolate dots, melted
Coffee – 10 ml/2 tsp/2 tsp coffee granules blended with 5 ml/1 tsp/1 tsp boiling water
Nuts – replace 25 g/1 oz/2 tbsp flour with finely ground nuts

Madeira Cake

A good, plain cake which can be made as an alternative to a light or rich fruit cake. It is firm and moist, can be flavoured to taste, and makes a good base for icing and decorating.

A madeira cake is traditionally used for decorative novelty cakes, as it provides a firm and lasting sponge base.

MADEIRA CAKE CHART

Cake Tin Sizes	15 cm/6 in Square	18 cm/7 in Square	20 cm/8 in Square	23 cm/9 in Square	25 cm/10 in Square	28 cm/11 in Square	30 cm/12 in Square
	18 cm/7 in Round	20 cm/8 in Round	23 cm/9 in Round	25 cm/10 in Round	28 cm/11 in Round	30 cm/12 in Round	33 cm/13 in Round
INGREDIENTS							
Plain (all-purpose) flour	225 g/ 8 oz/ 2 cups	350 g/ 12 oz/ 3 cups	450 g/ 1 lb/ 4 cups	500 g/ 1 lb 2 oz/ 4½ cups	575 g/ 1¼ lb/ 5 cups	675 g/ 1½ lb/ 6 cups	900 g/ 2 lb/ 8 cups
Baking powder	5 ml/ 1 tsp/ 1 tsp	7.5 ml/ 1½ tsp/ 1½ tsp	10 ml/ 2 tsp/ 2 tsp	12.5 ml/ 2½ tsp/ 2½ tsp	15 ml/ 3 tsp/ 3 tsp	17.5 ml/ 3½ tsp/ 3½ tsp	20 ml/ 4 tsp/ 4 tsp
Caster (superfine) sugar	175 g/ 6 oz/ ¾ cup	275 g/ 10 oz/ 1¼ cups	400 g/ 14 oz/ 1¾ cups	450 g/ 1 lb/ 2 cups	500 g/ 1 lb 2 oz/ 2¼ cups	625 g/ 1 lb 6 oz/ 2¾ cups	725 g/ 1 lb 10 oz/ 3¼ cups
Soft margarine	175 g/ 6 oz/ ¾ cup	275 g/ 10 oz/ 1¼ cups	400 g/ 14 oz/ 1¾ cups	450 g/ 1 lb/ 2 cups	500 g/ 1 lb 2 oz/ 2¼ cups	625 g/ 1 lb 6 oz/ 2¾ cups	725 g/ 1 lb 10 oz/ 3¼ cups
Size 3 eggs	3	5	7	8	10	12	13
Milk	30 ml/ 2 tbsp/ 2 tbsp	45 ml/ 3 tbsp/ 3 tbsp	55 ml/ 3½ tbsp/ 3½ tbsp	60 ml/ 4 tbsp/ 4 tbsp	70 ml/ 4½ tbsp/ 4½ tbsp	75 ml/ 5 tbsp/ 5 tbsp	85 ml/ 5½ tbsp/ 5½ tbsp
Approx. Cooking Time	1¼–1½ hours	1½–1¾ hours	1¾–2 hours	1¾–2 hours	2–2¼ hours	2¼–2½ hours	2½–2¾ hours

1 *Preheat the oven to 170°C/325°F/Gas 3.
Grease and line a deep cake tin (pan)
(see Lining Cake Tins [Pans]).*

2 *Sift flour and baking powder into a
mixing bowl. Add sugar, margarine,
eggs and milk. Mix together with a wooden
spoon, then beat for 1–2 minutes until
smooth and glossy. Alternatively, use an
electric mixer and beat for 1 minute only.*

3 *Add any flavourings desired and mix
until well blended.*

CHOICE OF FLAVOURINGS

The following amounts are for a
3-egg quantity cake. Increase the
suggested flavourings to suit the
quantities being made.

Cherry – 175 g/6 oz/1 scant cup
glacé cherries, halved

Citrus – replace milk with lemon,
orange or lime juice and 5 ml/1 tsp/1
tsp of grated lemon, orange or lime
rind

Coconut – 50 g/2 oz/1 cup desiccated
(shredded) coconut

Nuts – replace 125 g/4 oz/1 cup flour
with ground almonds, hazelnuts,
walnuts or pecan nuts

4 *Place the mixture into the prepared tin
(pan) and spread evenly. Give the tin
(pan) a sharp tap to remove any air pockets.
Make a depression in the centre of the
mixture to ensure a level surface.*

5 *Bake the cake in the centre of the oven.
Follow the chart cooking times,
according to the size of the cake. It is cooked
when the cake springs back when lightly
pressed in the centre.*

STORING

Leave the cake to cool in the tin
(pan), then remove and cool
completely on a wire rack. Wrap in
plastic wrap or foil and store in a
cool place until required.

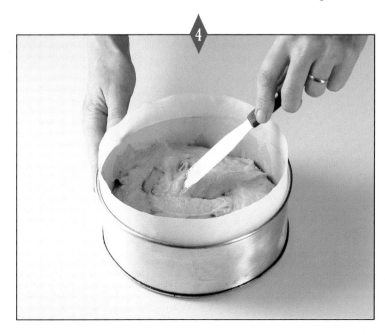

Rich Fruit Cake

This recipe makes a very moist rich cake suitable for any celebration. The cake can be made in stages, especially if time is short or if you are making more than one. It is easiest if the fruit is prepared and soaked overnight and the cake made the following day. Once the mixture is in the tin (pan), the surface may be covered with cling film (plastic wrap) and the cake stored in a cool place overnight if cooking is not possible on the day. The quantities have been carefully worked out so that the depth of each cake is the same. This is important when making several tiers for a wedding cake.

A classic rich fruit cake is traditionally used for christening cakes, as in the base for this delightful creation for a baby girl.

1 Into a large mixing bowl place the raisins, sultanas (golden raisins), currants, glacé cherries, mixed (candied) peel, flaked almonds, lemon rind and juice, brandy or sherry. Mix all the ingredients together until well blended, then cover the bowl with cling film (plastic wrap). Leave for several hours or overnight if required.

2 Pre-heat the oven to 140°C/275°F/Gas 1 and prepare a deep cake tin (see Lining Cake Tins [Pans]). Sift the flour and mixed spice into another mixing bowl. Add the ground almonds, sugar, butter, treacle (or molasses) and eggs. Mix together with a wooden spoon, then beat for 1–2 minutes until smooth and glossy. Alternatively, beat for 1 minute using an electric mixer.

3 Gradually add mixed fruit and fold into cake mixture using a plastic or wooden spatula until all the fruit has been evenly blended.

4 Spoon the mixture into the prepared tin (pan) and spread evenly. Give the container a few sharp bangs to level the mixture and to remove any air pockets. Smooth the surface with the back of a metal spoon, making a slight depression in the centre. The cake surface may be covered with cling film (plastic wrap) and left overnight in a cool place if required.

5 Bake the cake in the centre of the oven following the chart cooking time as a guide. Test the cake to see if it is cooked 30 minutes before the end of the cooking time. The cake should feel firm and, when a fine skewer is inserted into the centre, it should come out quite clean. If the cake is not cooked, retest it at 15-minute intervals. Remove the cake from the oven and allow it to cool in the tin (pan).

6 Turn the cake out of the tin (pan) but do not remove the lining paper as it helps to keep the moisture in. Spoon half quantity of brandy or sherry used in each cake over the top of the cooked cake and wrap in a double thickness of foil.

STORING

Store the cake in a cool, dry place on its base with the top uppermost for a week. Unwrap the cake and spoon over the remaining brandy or sherry. Rewrap well and invert the cake. Store it upside down, so the brandy or sherry moistens the top and helps to keep it flat.

The cake will store well for up to 3 months. If it is going to be stored for this length of time, add the brandy or sherry a little at a time at monthly intervals.

RICH FRUIT CAKE CHART

Cake Tin Sizes	12 cm/5 in Square	15 cm/6 in Square	18 cm/7 in Square	20 cm/8 in Square	23 cm/9 in Square	25 cm/10 in Square	28 cm/11 in Square	30 cm/12 in Square
	15 cm/6 in Round	18 cm/7 in Round	20 cm/8 in Round	23 cm/9 in Round	25 cm/10 in Round	28 cm/11 in Round	30 cm/12 in Round	33 cm/13 in Round

INGREDIENTS								
Raisins	200 g/ 7 oz/ 1⅓ cups	250 g/ 9 oz/ 1¾ cups	325 g/ 11 oz/ 2 cups	375 g/ 13 oz/ 2½ cups	425 g/ 15 oz/ 2⅔ cups	575 g/ 1¼ lb/ 3¾ cups	675 g/ 1½ lb/ 4½ cups	800 g/ 1¾ lb/ 5¼ cups
Sultanas (golden raisins)	125 g/ 4 oz/ ¾ cup	175 g/ 6 oz/ 1¼ cups	225 g/ 8 oz/ 1½ cups	275 g/ 10 oz/ 1⅔ cups	350 g/ 12 oz/ 2¼ cups	475 g/ 1 lb 1 oz/ 3¼ cups	600 g/ 1 lb 5 oz/ 4 cups	675 g/ 1½ lb/ 4½ cups
Currants	75 g/ 3 oz/ ⅔ cup	125 g/ 4 oz/ ¾ cup	175 g/ 6 oz/ 1¼ cups	225 g/ 8 oz/ 1⅔ cups	275 g/ 10 oz/ 2 cups	400 g/ 14 oz/ 3 cups	475 g/ 1 lb 1 oz/ 3½ cups	575 g/ 1¼ lb/ 4 cups
Glacé cherries, halved	75 g/ 3 oz/ ½ cup	75 g/ 3 oz/ ½ cup	150 g/ 5 oz/ 1 cup	175 g/ 6 oz/ 1 cup	200 g/ 7 oz/ 1⅓ cups	225 g/ 8 oz/ 1½ cups	275 g/ 10 oz/ 1⅔ cups	350 g/ 12 oz/ 2¼ cups
Mixed peel	25 g/ 1 oz/ ¼ cup	40 g/ 1½ oz/ ⅓ cup	50 g/ 2 oz/ ⅓ cup	75 g/ 3 oz/ ½ cup	125 g/ 4 oz/ ¾ cup	175 g/ 6 oz/ 1 cup	225 g/ 8 oz/ 1½ cups	275 g/ 10 oz/ 1⅔ cups
Flaked almonds	25 g/ 1 oz/ ¼ cup	40 g/ 1½ oz/ ⅓ cup	50 g/ 2 oz/ ½ cup	75 g/ 3 oz/ ¾ cup	125 g/ 4 oz/ 1 cup	175 g/ 6 oz/ 1⅔ cup	225 g/ 8 oz/ 2¼ cups	275 g/ 10 oz/ 2¾ cups
Lemon rind, coarsely grated	5 ml/ 1 tsp/ 1 tsp	7.5 ml/ 1½ tsp/ 1½ tsp	10 ml/ 2 tsp/ 2 tsp	12 ml/ 2½ tsp/ 2½ tsp	15 ml/ ½ fl oz/ 1 tbsp	25 ml/ 1½ tbsp/ 1½ tbsp	25 ml/ 1½ tbsp/ 1½ tbsp	30 ml/ 2 tbsp/ 2 tbsp
Lemon juice	15 ml/ 1 tbsp/ 1 tbsp	25 ml/ 1½ tbsp/ 1½ tbsp	30 ml/ 2 tbsp/ 2 tbsp	40 ml/ 2½ tbsp/ 2½ tbsp	45 ml/ 3 tbsp/ 3 tbsp	60 ml/ 4 tbsp/ 4 tbsp	75 ml/ 5 tbsp/ 5 tbsp	90 ml/ 6 tbsp/ 6 tbsp
Brandy or sherry	15 ml/ 1 tbsp/ 1 tbsp	30 ml/ 2 tbsp/ 2 tbsp	45 ml/ 3 tbsp/ 3 tbsp	60 ml/ 4 tbsp/ 4 tbsp	75 ml/ 5 tbsp/ 5 tbsp	90 ml/ 6 tbsp/ 6 tbsp	105 ml/ 7 tbsp/ 7 tbsp	120 ml/ 8 tbsp/ ½ cup
Plain (all-purpose) flour	175 g/ 6 oz/ 1½ cups	200 g/ 7 oz/ 1¾ cups	250 g/ 9 oz/ 2¼ cups	325 g/ 11 oz/ 2¾ cups	400 g/ 14 oz/ 3½ cups	500 g/ 1 lb 2 oz/ 4½ cups	625 g/ 1 lb 6 oz/ 5½ cups	725 g/ 1 lb 10 oz/ 6½ cups
Ground mixed spice	5 ml/ 1 tsp/ 1 tsp	7.5 ml/ 1½ tsp/ 1½ tsp	12 ml/ 2½ tsp/ 2½ tsp	15 ml/ 1 tbsp/ 1 tbsp	18 ml/ 1¼ tbsp/ 1¼ tbsp	25 ml/ 1½ tbsp/ 1½ tbsp	30 ml/ 2 tbsp/ 2 tbsp	70 ml/ 3½ tbsp/ 3½ tbsp
Ground almonds	25 g/ 1 oz/ ¼ cup	40 g/ 1½ oz/ ⅓ cup	65 g/ 2½ oz/ ⅔ cup	125 g/ 4 oz/ 1¼ cups	150 g/ 5 oz/ 1⅓ cups	225 g/ 8 oz/ 2¼ cups	275 g/ 10 oz/ 2¾ cups	350 g/ 12 oz/ 3⅓ cups
Dark brown sugar	125 g/ 4 oz/ ¾ cup	150 g/ 5 oz/ 1 cup	200 g/ 7 oz/ 1⅓ cups	250 g/ 9 oz/ 1⅔ cups	350 g/ 12 oz/ 2¼ cups	475 g/ 1 lb 1 oz/ 3⅓ cups	575 g/ 1¼ lb/ 3¾ cups	650 g/ 1 lb 7 oz/ 4½ cups
Butter, softened	125 g/ 4 oz/ ½ cup	150 g/ 5 oz/ ⅔ cup	200 g/ 7 oz/ 1 cup	250 g/ 9 oz/ 1¼ cups	350 g/ 12 oz/ 1½ cups	475 g/ 1 lb 1 oz/ 2¼ cups	575 g/ 1¼ lb/ 2½ cups	650 g/ 1 lb 7 oz/ 3 cups
Black treacle (or molasses)	10 ml/ ½ tbsp/ ½ tbsp	15 ml/ 1 tbsp/ 1 tbsp	25 ml/ 1½ tbsp/ 1½ tbsp	30 ml/ 2 tbsp/ 2 tbsp	40 ml/ 2½ tbsp/ 2½ tbsp	45 ml/ 3 tbsp/ 3 tbsp	55 ml/ 3½ tbsp/ 3½ tbsp	60 ml/ 4 tbsp/ 4 tbsp
Eggs	2	3	4	5	6	7	8	10
Approx. Cooking Time	2¼–2½ hours	2½–2¾ hours	3–3½ hours	3¼–3¾ hours	3¾–4¼ hours	4–4½ hours	4½–5¼ hours	5¼–5¾ hours

Light Fruit Cake

This is a very light moist fruit cake, which can be made to replace the rich version, if required. As there is less fruit in the cake, it has a tendency to dome during cooking, so ensure a deep depression is made in the centre. It will keep for up to one month once it has been marzipanned and iced.

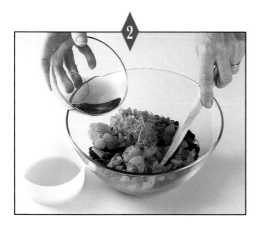

A light fruit teatime cake, simply topped with candied fruits and nuts, and glazed.

1 Preheat the oven to 140°C/275°F/Gas 1. Grease and line a deep cake tin (pan) (see Lining Cake Tins [Pans]).

2 Place the mixed dried fruit, peel, ginger, apricots, orange rind, juice and sherry in a large mixing bowl. Mix all the ingredients together until well blended.

3 Sift the flour, mixed spice and sugar into another mixing bowl, add the butter or margarine, and eggs. Mix together with a wooden spoon, then beat for 1–2 minutes until smooth and glossy. Alternatively, beat for 1 minute using an electric mixer.

4 Gradually add the mixed fruit and fold into the cake mixture, using a plastic spatula, until all the fruit is evenly mixed.

STORING

Remove the cake from oven and leave to cool in the tin (pan). Wrap in foil and store in a cool place for up to 4 weeks.

5 Spoon the mixture into the prepared cake tin (pan) and spread evenly. Give the tin (pan) a few sharp bangs to level the mixture and remove any air pockets. Smooth the surface with the back of a metal spoon, making a fairly deep depression in the centre.

6 Bake the cake in the centre of the oven. Use the chart cooking times as a guide, according to the size of cake you are making. Test the cake 15 minutes before the end of the given cooking time. If cooked, the cake should feel firm and when a fine skewer is inserted into the centre, it should come out quite clean. If the cake is not cooked, retest at 15 minute intervals.

LIGHT FRUIT CAKE CHART

Cake Tin Sizes	12 cm/5 in Square	15 cm/6 in Square	18 cm/7 in Square	20 cm/8 in Square	23 cm/9 in Square	25 cm/10 in Square	28 cm/11 in Square	30 cm/12 in Square
	15 cm/6 in Round	18 cm/7 in Round	20 cm/8 in Round	23 cm/9 in Round	25 cm/10 in Round	28 cm/11 in Round	30 cm/12 in Round	33 cm/13 in Round
INGREDIENTS								
Mixed dried fruit	275 g/ 10 oz/ 1⅔ cups	400 g/ 14 oz/ 1⅔ cups	450 g/ 1 lb/ 3 cups	675 g/ 1½ lb/ 4½ cups	900 g/ 2 lb/ 6 cups	1.1 kg/ 2½ lb/ 7½ cups	1.5 kg/ 3¼ lb/ 9¾ cups	1.8 kg/ 4 lb/ 12 cups
Mixed cut peel	25 g/ 1 oz/ ¼ cup	25 g/ 1 oz/ ¼ cup	25 g/ 1 oz/ ¼ cup	25 g/ 1 oz/ ¼ cup	50 g/ 2 oz/ ⅓ cup	75 g/ 3 oz/ ½ cup	150 g/ 5 oz/ 1 cup	175 g/ 6 oz/ 1 cup
Stem (preserved) ginger, chopped	25 g/ 1 oz/ ¼ cup	25 g/ 1 oz/ ¼ cup	50 g/ 2 oz/ ⅓ cup	75 g/ 3 oz/ ½ cup	125 g/ 4 oz/ ¾ cup	150 g/ 5 oz/ 1 cup	200 g/ 7 oz/ 1¼ cups	225 g/ 8 oz/ 1½ cups
Dried apricots	25 g/ 1 oz/ ¼ cup	25 g/ 1 oz/ ¼ cup	50 g/ 2 oz/ ½ cup	75 g/ 3 oz/ ¾ cup	125 g/ 4 oz/ 1 cup	150 g/ 5 oz/ 1¼ cups	175 g/ 6 oz/ 1½ cups	225 g/ 8 oz/ 2 cups
Orange rind, coarsely grated	5 ml/ 1 tsp/ 1 tsp	7.5 ml/ 1½ tsp/ 1½ tsp	10 ml/ 2 tsp/ 2 tsp	15 ml/ 1 tbsp/ 1 tbsp	20 ml/ 4 tsp/ 4 tsp	25 ml/ 5 tsp/ 5 tsp	30 ml/ 2 tbsp/ 2 tbsp	40 ml/ 8 tsp/ 8 tsp
Orange juice	15 ml/ 1 tbsp/ 1 tbsp	25 ml/ 1½ tbsp/ 1½ tbsp	30 ml/ 2 tbsp/ 2 tbsp	40 ml/ 2½ tbsp/ 2½ tbsp	45 ml/ 3 tbsp/ 3 tbsp	55 ml/ 3½ tbsp/ 3½ tbsp	70 ml/ 4½ tbsp/ 4½ tbsp	75 ml/ 5 tbsp/ 5 tbsp
Sherry	15 ml/ 1 tbsp/ 1 tbsp	20 ml/ 1½ tbsp/ 1½ tbsp	30 ml/ 2 tbsp/ 2 tbsp	40 ml/ 2½ tbsp/ 2½ tbsp	45 ml/ 3 tbsp/ 3 tbsp	55 ml/ 3½ tbsp/ 3½ tbsp	70 ml/ 4½ tbsp/ 4½ tbsp	85 ml/ 5½ tbsp/ 5½ tbsp
Plain (all-purpose) flour	225 g/ 8 oz/ 2 cups	275 g/ 10 oz/ 2½ cups	350 g/ 12 oz/ 3 cups	450 g/ 1 lb/ 4 cups	575 g/ 1¼ lb/ 5 cups	675 g/ 1½ lb/ 7 cups	900 g/ 2 lb/ 7 cups	1.1 kg/ 2½ lb/ 9 cups
Ground mixed spice	5 ml/ 1 tsp/ 1 tsp	7.5 ml/ 1½ tsp/ 1½ tsp	10 ml/ 2 tsp/ 2 tsp	15 ml/ 1 tbsp/ 1 tbsp	20 ml/ 4 tsp/ 4 tsp	25 ml/ 5 tsp/ 5 tsp	30 ml/ 2 tbsp/ 2 tbsp	40 ml/ 8 tsp/ 8 tsp
Light soft brown sugar	175 g/ 6 oz/ 1 cup	225 g/ 8 oz/ 1 cup	275 g/ 10 oz/ 1⅔ cups	400 g/ 14 oz/ 2½ cups	475 g/ 1 lb 1 oz/ 3¼ cups	575 g/ 1¼ lb/ 3¾ cups	775 g/ 1 lb 11 oz/ 5 cups	975 g/ 2 lb 2 oz/ 6⅓ cups
Butter or margarine, softened	175 g/ 6 oz/ ¾ cup	225 g/ 8 oz/ 1 cup	275 g/ 10 oz/ 1¼ cups	400 g/ 14 oz/ 1¾ cups	475 g/ 1 lb 1 oz/ 2¼ cups	575 g/ 1¼ lb/ 2½ cups	775 g/ 1 lb 11 oz/ 3¼ cups	975 g/ 2 lb 2 oz/ 4¼ cups
Size 3 eggs	3	4	4	5	6	7	9	11
Approx. Cooking Time	2¼–2½ hours	2½–2¾ hours	2¾–3¼ hours	3¼–3¾ hours	3½–4 hours	4–4½ hours	4½–4¾ hours	5–5½ hours

Genoese Sponge Cake

This whisked sponge cake has a firmer texture due to the addition of butter and is suitable for cutting into layers for gateaux, or as a base for a celebration cake.

INGREDIENTS

- 4 eggs
- 125 g/4 oz/½ cup caster (superfine) sugar
- 75 g/3 oz/⅓ cup + 3 tsp unsalted butter, melted and cooled slightly
- 75 g/3 oz/¾ cup + 6 tsp plain (all-purpose) flour

Genoese sponge is the classic whisked sponge, suitable for plain and highly fancy cakes; here it is deliciously decorated with apricots and praline-coated nuts.

1 *Preheat the oven to 180°C/350°F/Gas 4. Prepare the tin (pan) according to the recipe.*

2 *Whisk eggs and caster (superfine) sugar together in a heatproof bowl until thoroughly blended. Place the bowl over a saucepan of simmering water and whisk the mixture until thick and pale.*

3 *Remove the bowl from the saucepan and continue whisking until the mixture is cool and leaves a thick trail on the surface when beaters are lifted.*

CHOICE OF FLAVOURINGS

Citrus – 10 ml/2 tsp/2 tsp finely grated orange, lemon or lime rind
Chocolate – 50 g/2 oz/2 squares plain (semisweet) chocolate, melted
Coffee – 10 ml/2 tsp/2 tsp coffee granules, dissolved in 5 ml/1 tsp/1 tsp boiling water

4 *Pour the butter carefully into the mixture, leaving any sediment behind.*

5 *Sift flour over surface and, using a plastic spatula, carefully fold the flour, butter and any flavourings into the mixture until smooth and evenly blended.*
   Place the mixture into the prepared tin (pan), tilt to level and bake as required.

SIMPLE ICINGS (FROSTINGS)

Special Equipment for Icing

Before embarking on any form of cake icing or decorating, it is necessary to have a selection of icing equipment to achieve good results.

1 Straight edge
2 Turntable
3 Fine nozzles in various sizes and designs
4 Acrylic rolling pin
5 Acrylic dowels
6 Large nozzles in various designs
7 Greaseproof (wax) paper piping bags
8 Cake pillars
9 Florists' wire
10 Flower cutters
11 Stamens
12 Florists' tape
13 Acrylic rolling board

14 Brushes
15 Smoother for sugarpaste (fondant) covered cakes
16 Biscuit (cookie) and aspic cutters
17 Patterned and plain side scrapers
18 Nozzle brush
19 Nylon piping bags
20 Flower nail

Turntable – the most essential piece of equipment for easy movement of cakes while icing and decorating. Although expensive, it will last for ever and is obtainable from most kitchen shops or cake-icing specialists. The turntable should revolve smoothly for applying royal icing to a round cake.

Straight Edge – made from metal, stainless steel is the best. It is rigid and will not scratch or bend when using it to level the top of a cake to obtain flat, smooth royal icing.

Side Scraper – made from plastic or stainless steel and used for smoothing the icing on the sides of a cake. The plastic ones are more flexible and easier to use.

Patterned Side Scrapers – come in a variety of designs and are ideal for finishing the sides of an iced cake in many different patterns.

Muslin (Cheesecloth) – ideal for covering a bowl of royal icing to prevent a skin forming. As it is white it will not impart any colour.

Brushes – fine artists' brushes, available from cake-icing specialists, have many uses for painting flowers and plaques with food colouring; also useful when making icing run-outs.

Flower Nail – can be homemade from a cork and nail. Otherwise buy one from a kitchen shop or a cake-icing specialist. It is invaluable for piping flowers.

Small Biscuit (Cookie) or Aspic Cutters – these are used for cutting out various shapes from sugarpaste, marzipan, chocolate or fruit rinds to use as decorations. They also come as numbers and letters. Tiny cutters are available for making cut-out flowers from sugarpaste.

Tweezers – these are indispensable for delicate work; buy a pair with rounded ends.

Stamens – can be found in different colours and finishes from cake-decorating specialists. They are used in the centre of moulded and cut-out sugar flowers.

Dowel – different sizes of wooden dowel are useful for placing leaves and petals over to dry, giving them a more realistic shape. Acrylic dowels are also used to support the tiers of a cake covered in sugarpaste.

Florists' wire and tape – these come in various gauges and colours and are available from cake-icing specialists. Use to wire sugar flowers onto stems, or to bind stems together to form a flower spray.

Piping Bags – made in a variety of materials; the nylon ones are soft and flexible for cream, meringue and icing.

Use a nylon piping bag and a large star-shaped nozzle to pipe a decorative border with fresh cream.

Available in small, medium and large sizes, to be fitted with various sizes of nozzles. Greaseproof (wax) paper piping bags can be made easily and used with a variety of straight-sided nozzles, or even without a nozzle.

Large Nozzles – buy a simple selection of small to medium star metal meringue nozzles. These will fit the nylon piping bags and also large homemade greaseproof (wax) paper piping bags. They are ideal for piping cream, meringues and butter icing.

Fine Nozzles – straight-sided metal nozzles are the best type to buy as they fit into homemade greaseproof (wax) paper piping bags. They are available in many different designs and sizes.

Nozzle Brush – essential for cleaning nozzles without bending or misshaping the ends.

Icing Syringes – usually available as a set, with a selection of nozzles, and are ideal for simple piping.

Acrylic Rolling Pin and Board – non-stick, they are ideal for rolling out small pieces of sugarpaste or marzipan decorations.

Cake Pillars – these are available in plastic rounds, squares and octagonals, usually with a hole through the centre to cover the acrylic sticks used to support a wedding cake covered with sugarpaste. Plaster pillars have a clean, crisp finish for royal-iced wedding cakes.

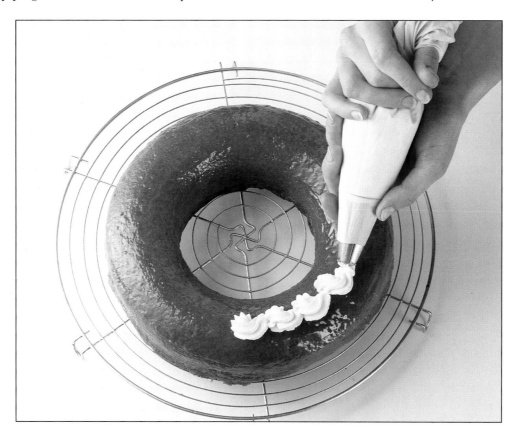

Butter Icing

This most popular and well-known icing is made quickly with butter and icing (confectioners) sugar. Add your choice of flavourings and colourings to vary the cake.

INGREDIENTS

Makes 450 g/1 lb/1 lb
- *125 g/4 oz/¹/₂ cup unsalted butter, softened*
- *225 g/8 oz/2 cups icing (confectioners) sugar, sifted*
- *10 ml/2 tsp/2 tsp milk*
- *5 ml/1 tsp/1 tsp vanilla essence (extract)*

Butter icing is a quick and attractive topping for a cake.

1 *Place the butter in a bowl. Using a wooden spoon or an electric mixer, beat until light and fluffy.*

2 *Stir in the icing (confectioners) sugar, milk and vanilla essence (extract), and/ or flavourings until evenly mixed, then beat well until light and smooth.*

3 *Spread the icing over the cake with a metal palette knife (spatula).*

CHOICE OF FLAVOURINGS

Citrus – replace milk and vanilla essence (extract) with orange, lemon or lime juice and 10 ml/2 tsp/2 tsp finely grated orange, lemon or lime rind. Omit the rind if the icing is to be piped.

Chocolate – 15 ml/1 tbsp/1 tbsp cocoa powder blended with 15 ml/1 tbsp/1 tbsp boiling water, cooled
Coffee – 10 ml/2 tsp/2 tsp coffee granules blended with 15 ml/1 tbsp/1 tbsp boiling water, cooled

Crème au Beurre

This icing takes a little more time to make, but it is well worth it. The rich, smooth, light texture makes it suitable for spreading, filling or piping onto special cakes and gateaux. Use it as soon as it is made for best results, or keep it at room temperature for a few hours. Do not rebeat or it will curdle.

INGREDIENTS

Makes 350 g/12 oz/¾ lb
- 60 ml/4 tbsp/4 tbsp water
- 75 g/3 oz/⅓ cup caster (superfine) sugar
- 2 egg yolks
- 150 g/5 oz/⅔ cup unsalted butter, softened

Creme au beurre is a sophisticated filling and topping for a cake.

1 *Place the water in a small saucepan, bring to boil, remove the saucepan from the heat and stir in the sugar. Heat gently until the sugar has completely dissolved. Remove the spoon.*

2 *Boil rapidly until mixture becomes syrupy, or until the 'thread' stage is reached. To test, remove the pan from heat, place a little syrup on the back of a dry teaspoon. Press a second teaspoon onto the syrup and gently pull apart. The syrup should form a fine thread. If not, return the saucepan to heat, boil rapidly and retest a minute later.*

3 *Whisk the egg yolks together in a bowl. Continue whisking while slowly adding the sugar syrup in a steady stream. Whisk until mixture becomes thick, pale and cool, and leaves a trail on surface when the beaters are lifted.*

CHOICE OF FLAVOURINGS

Citrus – replace water with orange, lemon or lime juice and 10 ml/2 tsp/2 tsp finely grated orange, lemon or lime rind

4 *Beat the butter in a separate bowl until light and fluffy. Add the egg mixture gradually, beating well after each addition, until thick and fluffy.*
  Fold in the chosen flavouring, using a spatula, until evenly blended.

Chocolate – 50 g/2 oz/2 squares plain (semisweet) chocolate, melted
Coffee – 10 ml/2 tsp/2 tsp coffee granules, dissolved in 5 ml/1 tsp/1 tsp boiling water, cooled

American Frosting

A light marshmallow icing which crisps on the outside when left to dry, this versatile frosting may be swirled or peaked into a soft coating.

INGREDIENTS

Makes 350 g/12 oz/¾ lb
- *1 egg white*
- *30 ml/2 tbsp/2 tbsp water*
- *15 ml/1 tbsp/1 tbsp golden syrup (light corn syrup)*
- *5 ml/1 tsp/1 tsp cream of tartar*
- *175 g/6 oz/1 cup icing (confectioners) sugar, sifted*

American frosting makes a light, fluffy yet crisp topping, its soft white contrasting well with chocolate caraque.

1 *Place the egg white, water, golden syrup (light corn syrup) and cream of tartar in a heatproof bowl. Whisk together until thoroughly blended.*

2 *Stir the icing (confectioners) sugar into the mixture and place the bowl over a saucepan of simmering water. Whisk until the mixture becomes thick and white.*

3 *Remove the bowl from the saucepan and continue to whisk the frosting until cool and thick, and the mixture stands up in soft peaks.*

4 *Use immediately to fill or cover cakes.*

Glacé Icing

An instant icing for quickly finishing the tops of large or small cakes, this is also used to make feathered icing by introducing a second, coloured, icing to obtain the feathered design.

Makes 350 g/12 oz/³⁄₄ lb
- 225 g/8 oz/1¹⁄₂ cups icing (confectioners) sugar
- 30–45 ml/2–3 tbsp/2–3 tbsp hot water
- food colouring (optional)

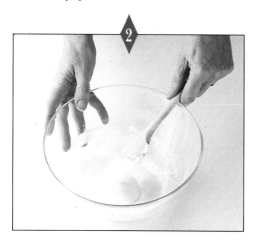

1 Sift the icing (confectioners) sugar into a bowl. Using a wooden spoon, gradually stir in enough water to obtain the consistency of thick cream.

2 Beat until white and smooth, and the icing thickly coats the back of a wooden spoon. Colour with a few drops of food colouring if desired.

3 Use immediately to cover the top of the cake.

CHOICE OF FLAVOURINGS

Citrus – replace the water with orange, lemon or lime juice
Chocolate – sift 10 ml/2 tsp/2 tsp cocoa powder with the icing (confectioners) sugar
Coffee – replace the water with strong, liquid coffee

FEATHER ICING
1 Colour one-third glacé icing a pale shade with food colouring. Place in a greaseproof (wax) paper piping bag. Snip off point.
2 Quickly spread the cake surface evenly and smoothly with white glacé icing. Immediately pipe coloured lines of icing, evenly spaced, on top of the white icing.
3 Draw a cocktail stick lightly across the lines of icing in alternate directions, evenly spaced, to form a feather pattern (see above).

COBWEB ICING
1 Pipe circles of glacé icing over the top of the cake and draw a cocktail stick from centre to edge in one direction to make a cobweb design.
2 To vary the pattern, pipe dots of icing evenly over the surface of the cake. Draw a cocktail stick through the dots to make another design.

Butterscotch Frosting

This is a richly-flavoured frosting, using brown sugar and treacle (molasses). It is useful for coating any sponge cake to impart a smooth or swirled finish.

INGREDIENTS

Makes 675 g/1½ lb/1½ lb
- 75 g/3 oz/⅓ cup unsalted butter
- 45 ml/3 tbsp/3 tbsp milk
- 25 g/1 oz/2 tbsp soft light brown sugar
- 15 ml/1 tbsp/1 tbsp black treacle (or molasses)
- 350 g/12 oz/2¼ cups icing (confectioners) sugar, sifted

Butterscotch frosting is deliciously caramel-flavoured and an unusual alternative for coating a cake.

1 *Place the butter, milk, sugar and treacle (or molasses) in a heatproof bowl over a saucepan of simmering water. Stir occasionally, using a wooden spoon, until the butter and sugar have melted.*

2 *Remove the bowl from the saucepan. Stir in the icing (confectioners) sugar, then beat until smooth and glossy.*

3 *Pour immediately over the cake for a smooth finish, or allow to cool for a thicker spreading consistency.*

CHOICE OF FLAVOURINGS

Citrus – replace treacle (molasses) with golden syrup (light corn syrup) and add 10 ml/2 tsp/2 tsp of finely grated orange, lemon or lime rind
Chocolate – sift 15 ml/1 tbsp/1 tbsp cocoa powder with icing (confectioners) sugar
Coffee – replace the treacle (molasses) with 15 ml/1 tbsp/1 tbsp coffee granules

Chocolate Fudge Icing

A rich glossy icing which sets like chocolate fudge, it is versatile enough to smoothly coat, swirl or pipe, depending on the temperature of the icing when it is used.

INGREDIENTS

Makes 450 g/1 lb/1 lb

- 125 g/4 oz/4 squares plain (semisweet) chocolate
- 50 g/2 oz/¼ cup unsalted butter
- 1 egg, beaten
- 175 g/6 oz/1 cup icing (confectioners) sugar, sifted

Chocolate fudge icing is smooth and sumptuous, with a rich dark colour that contrasts beautifully with fresh flowers in a simple but effective decoration.

1 *Place the chocolate and butter in a heatproof bowl over a saucepan of hot water.*

2 *Stir occasionally with a wooden spoon until melted. Add the egg and beat until smooth.*

3 *Remove the bowl from the saucepan and stir in the icing (confectioners) sugar, then beat until smooth and glossy.*

4 *Pour immediately over the cake for a smooth finish, or leave to cool for a thicker spreading or piping consistency as here.*

Glossy Chocolate Icing

A rich smooth glossy icing, this can be made with plain (semisweet) or milk chocolate.

INGREDIENTS

Makes 350 g/12 oz/³/₄ lb
- 175 g/6 oz/6 squares plain (semi-sweet) chocolate
- 150 ml/¹/₄ pt/²/₃ cup single (light) cream

Glossy chocolate icing is the perfect setting for chocolate-dipped fruits and chocolate leaves.

1 *Break up the chocolate into small pieces and place in a medium-sized saucepan with the cream.*

2 *Heat gently, stirring occasionally, until the chocolate has melted and the mixture is smooth.*

3 *Allow the icing to cool until it is thick enough to coat the back of a wooden spoon. Use it at this stage for a smooth glossy icing as here, or allow it to thicken to obtain a swirled pattern icing.*

Meringue Frosting

A lightly-whisked meringue cooked over hot water and combined with softly beaten butter, this icing may be flavoured with the suggested flavourings, and should be used directly it is made.

INGREDIENTS

Makes 450 g/1 lb/1 lb
- *2 egg whites*
- *125 g/4 oz/³/₄ cup icing (confectioners) sugar, sifted*
- *150 g/5 oz/²/₃ cup unsalted butter, softened*

Meringue frosting creates a fluffy coating for cakes that can be spread or peaked to create a variety of effects.

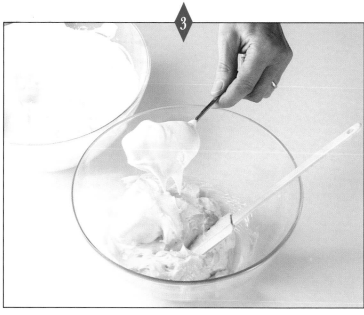

1 *Whisk egg whites in a clean, heatproof bowl, add the icing (confectioners) sugar and gently whisk to mix well.*

2 *Place the bowl over a saucepan of simmering water and whisk until thick and white. Remove the bowl from the saucepan, continue to whisk until it is cool and the meringue stands up in soft peaks.*

CHOICE OF FLAVOURINGS

Fold in the chosen flavourings, using a spatula, until evenly blended.

Citrus – 10 ml/2 tsp/2 tsp finely grated orange, lemon or lime rind
Chocolate – 50 g/2 oz/2 squares plain (semisweet) chocolate, melted
Coffee – 10 ml/2 tsp/2 tsp coffee granules blended with 5 ml/1 tsp/1 tsp boiling water, cooled

3 *Beat the butter in a separate bowl until light and fluffy. Add the meringue gradually, beating well after each addition, until thick and fluffy. Use immediately for coating, filling and piping cakes.*

MARZIPAN

Marzipan is a pliable paste made from ground almonds and a mixture of sugars. The consistency, texture and colour varies, depending upon how the paste is made, but the end result is used for covering cakes to give a smooth, flat surface before applying royal icing or sugarpaste.

Homemade marzipan has a much richer taste than the commercial variety and can be easily made in manageable quantities. Do take care not to overknead or handle the marzipan too much when making it, as this encourages the oils from the ground almonds to flow. They will eventually seep through the iced surface of the cake, causing staining.

Ready-made marzipan is available in white and yellow varieties. Use the white marzipan for all cakes as it is the most

Marzipan is the classic covering for the traditional Easter Simnel cake, which contains a central layer of marzipan as well as marzipan decoration.

popular and reliable type to use, especially when cakes are being iced in pastel shades or in white. The yellow marzipan has added food colouring but may be used for covering rich fruit cakes. Use with care, however, the yellow colour can show through if the icing is thinly applied, or may cause yellow staining. This marzipan does not take food colourings as well as white marzipan when used for modelling work.

Always use fresh, pliable marzipan to obtain the best results, especially for covering a cake. Be sure to dry the marzipanned cake before applying the icing. Set marzipan ensures a good cake shape during icing and prevents any moisture seeping through from the cake and staining the iced surface.

Always store the marzipanned cake on a clean cakeboard in a cake box in a warm, dry room.

Homemade Marzipan

INGREDIENTS

Makes 450 g/1 lb/1 lb
- 225 g/8 oz/2¼ cups ground almonds
- 125 g/4 oz/½ cup caster (superfine) sugar
- 125 g/4 oz/¾ cup icing (confectioners) sugar, sieved (sifted)
- 5 ml/1 tsp/1 tsp lemon juice
- few drops almond flavouring
- 1 (size 4) egg, or 1 (size 2) egg white

Marzipan is extremely versatile; here it has been used in place of icing for this unusual Christmas cake.

1 *Place the ground almonds, caster (superfine) and icing (confectioners) sugars into a bowl. Stir until evenly mixed.*

2 *Make a 'well' in the centre and add the lemon juice, almond flavouring and enough egg or egg white to mix to a soft but firm dough, using a wooden spoon.*

3 *Form the marzipan into a ball. Lightly dust a surface with icing (confectioners) sugar and knead the marzipan until smooth and free from cracks.*

4 *Wrap in cling film (plastic wrap) or store in a polythene (polyethylene) bag until ready for use. Tint with food colouring if required, and use for moulding shapes or covering cakes.*

MARZIPAN CHART

Cake Tin Sizes	12 cm/5 in Square	15 cm/6 in Square	18 cm/7 in Square	20 cm/8 in Square	23 cm/9 in Square	25 cm/10 in Square	28 cm/11 in Square	30 cm/12 in Square
	15 cm/6 in Round	18 cm/7 in Round	20 cm/8 in Round	23 cm/9 in Round	25 cm/10 in Round	28 cm/11 in Round	30 cm/12 in Round	33 cm/13 in Round
QUANTITIES								
Apricot glaze	25 ml/ 1½ tbsp/ 1½ tbsp	30 ml/ 2 tbsp/ 2 tbsp	40 ml/ 2½ tbsp/ 2½ tbsp	45 ml/ 3 tbsp/ 3 tbsp	55 ml/ 3½ tbsp/ 3½ tbsp	60 ml/ 4 tbsp/ 4 tbsp	75 ml/ 4½ tbsp/ 4½ tbsp	75 ml/ 5 tbsp/ 5 tbsp
Marzipan	450 g/ 1 lb/ 1 lb	675 g/ 1½ lb/ 1½ lb	800 g/ 1¾ lb/ 1¾ lb	900 g/ 2 lb/ 2 lb	1.1 kg/ 2½ lb/ 2½ lb	1.5 kg/ 3¼ lb/ 3¼ lb	1.8 kg/ 4 lb/ 4 lb	1.9 kg/ 4¼ lb/ 4¼ lb

How to Marzipan a Cake for Royal Icing

1 Unwrap the cake and remove the lining paper. Place the cake on a cakeboard and roll the top with a rolling pin to flatten slightly.

2 Brush the top of the cake with apricot glaze. Lightly dust a surface with icing (confectioners) sugar.

3 Using two-thirds of the marzipan, knead it into a round. Roll out to a 5 mm/¼ in thickness to match the shape of the top of the cake, allowing an extra 2 cm/¾ in all around. Make sure the marzipan moves freely before inverting the cake onto the centre of the marzipan.

4 Trim off the excess marzipan to within 1 cm/½ in of the cake. Using a small flexible metal palette knife (spatula), push the marzipan level to the side of the cake, until all the marzipan is neat around the edge of the cake.

5 Invert the cake and place in the centre of the cakeboard. Brush the sides with apricot glaze. Knead the trimmings together, taking care not to include any crumbs from the cake.

6 Measure and cut a piece of string the length of the side of the cake. Measure and cut another piece of string the depth of the side of the cake from the board to the top.

7 Roll out the marzipan to 5 mm/¼ in thickness. Cut out one side piece for a round cake and four pieces for a square cake, to match the measured string. Knead the trimmings together and re-roll.

8 Carefully fit the marzipan onto the side of the cake and smooth the joins with a metal palette knife (spatula). Leave in a warm, dry place for at least 24 hours before icing.

How to Marzipan a Cake for Sugarpaste (Fondant Icing)

APRICOT GLAZE

It is always a good idea to make a large quantity of apricot glaze, especially when making celebration cakes. Use for brushing the cakes before applying the marzipan, or for glazing fruits on gateaux and cakes.

INGREDIENTS

Makes 450 g/1 lb/1 lb
- *450 g/1 lb/1½ cups apricot jam*
- *45 ml/3 tbsp/3 tbsp water*

1 *Place jam and water into a saucepan, heat gently, stirring occasionally until melted. Boil rapidly for 1 minute, then strain through a sieve (strainer).*

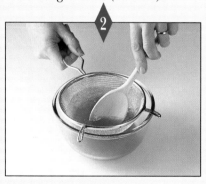

2 *Rub through as much fruit as possible, using a wooden spoon. Discard the skins left in the sieve (strainer).*

STORING

Pour the glaze into a clean, hot jar, seal with a clean lid and cool. Refrigerate for up to 2 months.

1 *Unwrap the cake and remove the lining paper. Place the cake on a cakeboard and roll the top with a rolling pin to flatten slightly.*

2 *Brush the top and sides of the cake with apricot glaze (see above), and dust the surface lightly with sieved (sifted) icing (confectioners) sugar.*

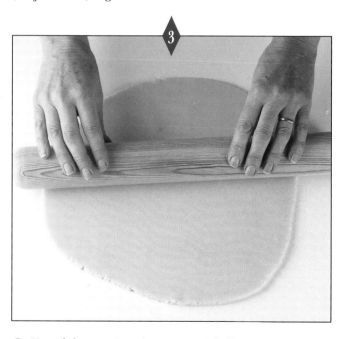

3 *Knead the marzipan into a smooth ball. Roll out to a 5 mm/¼ in thickness, to match the shape of the cake, and large enough to cover the top and sides, about 5–7.5 cm/2–3 in larger. Make sure the marzipan moves freely, then roll the marzipan loosely around the rolling pin.*

4 Place the supported marzipan over the cake and carefully unroll so that the marzipan falls evenly over the cake. Working from the centre of the cake, carefully smooth the marzipan over the top and down the sides, lifting the edges slightly to allow the marzipan to fit at the base of the cake without stretching or tearing the top edge.

5 Using a sharp knife, trim the excess marzipan from the base of the cake, cutting down on to the board.

6 Using clean, dry hands, gently rub the top of the cake in circular movements to make a smooth glossy finish to the marzipan.

7 Leave in a warm, dry place for at least 2 hours before covering with sugarpaste (fondant).

ROYAL ICING

Royal icing is the classic choice for all wedding, christening and other formal iced cakes, and is highly durable once dried.

A royal-iced cake has always been the traditional way of producing an English wedding or celebration cake. It is instantly recognizable by the classical lines and smooth finish, which certainly gives it a regal appearance.

To produce a beautifully royal-iced cake, it is essential to make the icing light and glossy in texture and of the correct consistency. Then with patience and practice, a good result can be achieved.

Everything must be spotless when making royal icing, and as dust-free as possible. Small particles can get into the icing and will come to the surface on a flat coat, or even cause the piping tubes to block.

Fresh egg whites or dried egg albumen may be used to make the icing – both produce good results. A little lemon juice helps to strengthen the albumen in fresh egg whites, but care must be taken not to add too much. Too much will make the icing short, causing it to break during piping, and making it difficult to obtain a smooth flat finish. Do not add glycerine to egg albumen as it does not set as hard as fresh egg-white icing.

Adding the icing (confectioners) sugar must be a gradual process, requiring plenty of mixing rather than beating during each addition of sugar, until the required consistency is reached. The icing should be light in texture and glossy in appearance.

Royal icing with too much icing (confectioners) sugar added too quickly will give a dull, heavy result and be grainy in appearance. It will be difficult to work with and, as it sets, will appear chalky and dull instead of sparkling white. It will also be difficult to pipe, soon becoming short and breaking off easily.

The prepared icing must be covered to exclude all air and prevent the surface from drying. Use damp cling film (plastic wrap) to seal the surface, or fill an airtight container to the top with icing. Covering with a damp cloth is fine for short periods but if left overnight the icing will absorb all the moisture, causing the consistency to be diluted.

If the icing is too stiff, add egg white or reconstituted egg albumen to make it softer. If the icing is too soft, gradually stir in more icing (confectioners) sugar for the required consistency.

Work from a small quantity of icing in a separate bowl from the main batch, covering it with damp muslin (cheesecloth) during use and keeping it well scraped down. If this small amount does become dry and cracked, at least it will not affect the whole batch of royal icing.

Royal Icing 1

This icing made with fresh egg whites is traditionally used to cover celebration cakes. Depending upon its consistency, it may be used for flat icing, peaked icing or piping designs on to cakes.

INGREDIENTS

Makes 450 g/1 lb/1½ cups
- *2 egg whites*
- *1.5 ml/¼ tsp/¼ tsp lemon juice*
- *450 g/1 lb/3 cups icing (confectioners) sugar, sieved (sifted)*
- *5 ml/1 tsp/1 tsp glycerine*

Peaked royal icing has been used to coat little fruit cakes for a witty and attractive festive gift.

Royal Icing Consistencies

The consistency of royal icing varies for different uses. Stiff icing is necessary for piping, slightly softer for flat icing or peaked icing, and slacker for run-outs.

PIPING CONSISTENCY
When a wooden spoon is drawn out of the icing, it should form a fine, sharp point, termed as 'sharp peak'. This consistency flows easily for piping but retains a definite shape produced by the nozzle.

FLAT OR PEAKED ICING CONSISTENCY
When the spoon is drawn out of the icing it should form a fine point which curves over at the end, termed as 'soft peak'. This consistency spreads smoothly and creates a flat finish, but also pulls up into sharp or soft peaks.

RUN-OUTS
Use soft peak consistency to pipe the outlines, and thick cream consistency to fill in the shapes. This consistency flows to fill in the run-outs, but holds a rounded shape within the piped lines.

1 *Place the egg whites and lemon juice in a clean bowl. Using a clean wooden spoon, stir to break up the egg whites. Add sufficient icing (confectioners) sugar and mix well to form the consistency of unwhipped cream.*

2 *Continue mixing and adding small quantities of sugar every few minutes, until the desired consistency has been reached. Mix well after each addition of sugar.*

3 *Stir in the glycerine until the icing is well blended.*

Royal Icing 2

Dried powdered egg white is known as egg albumen and may be used in place of fresh egg whites for royal icing. Simply blend the egg albumen with water to reconstitute it as directed on the packet, then add the icing (confectioners) sugar. The dried egg white is more convenient to use as there are no egg yolks to dispose of and it produces a good, light, glossy icing which is easy to handle. Used as flat icing for tiered cakes, it sets hard enough to support the weight of the cakes, but still cuts easily without being brittle. This icing is suitable for flat or peaked icing, piping and run-outs.

Note Use double-strength dried egg albumen for run-outs so that the run-out pieces set hard enough to remove from the paper.

INGREDIENTS

Makes 450 g/1 lb/1½ cups
- *15 g/½ oz/1 tbsp dried egg albumen*
- *90 ml/6 tbsp/6 tbsp tepid water*
- *450 g/1 lb/3 cups icing (confectioners) sugar, sieved (sifted)*

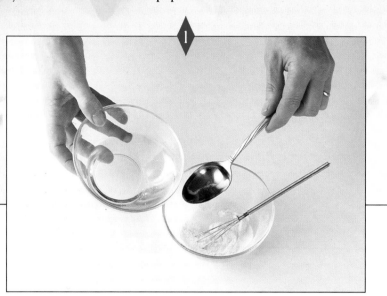

1 Put the egg albumen into a clean bowl. Using a clean spoon, gradually stir in the water and blend well together until the liquid is smooth and free from lumps.

2 Add sufficient icing (confectioners) sugar and mix well to form the consistency of unwhipped cream. Continue mixing and adding small quantities of sugar every few minutes until the desired consistency has been reached, mixing well after each addition of sugar. The icing should be smooth, glossy and light, almost like a cold meringue in texture, but not aerated. Do not add too much sugar too quickly as this will produce a dull, heavy icing which is difficult to handle.

3 Allow the icing to settle before using it; cover the surface with a piece of damp cling film (plastic wrap) and seal well, excluding all the air.

4 Stir the icing thoroughly before use as this will disperse the air bubbles, then adjust the consistency if necessary by adding more sieved (sifted) icing (confectioners) sugar or reconstituted egg albumen.

To Royal-ice a Round Cake

1 *The method for royal icing a round cake is the same as for icing a square cake, but easier as there are only two surfaces to ice – the top and side. Following the instructions for royal icing a square cake, spread the top of the cake evenly with icing.*

2 *Draw a straight edge across the top; repeat if unsatisfactory. Neaten the top edge and leave the icing to dry for at least two hours in a warm, dry place.*

3 *Spread the side of the cake evenly with icing and leave the cake on the turntable. Neaten the top edge with a metal palette knife (spatula).*

4 *Hold the side scraper firmly on to the side of the cake, resting on the cakeboard. Hold the cakeboard and turntable with one hand and the scraper with the other; turn the cake and turntable continuously in one revolution in one direction and at the same time hold the side scraper against the icing, pulling it towards you in the opposite direction to smooth the icing. Draw the side scraper gradually off the cake.*

5 *Neaten the top edge and the cakeboard edge. Leave the cake to dry before repeating the procedure to cover the cake with three or four thin layers of icing. Use a slightly softer consistency of icing for the final layer.*

To Royal-ice a Round Cakeboard

1 When the icing is completely dry, place the cake on to the turntable, and ensure the cakeboard is free from dry icing. Spread a thin layer of icing onto the cakeboard, neaten the edge of the board with a palette knife (spatula).

2 Place the side scraper onto the board and turn the cake and turntable in one revolution, drawing the side edge towards you to smooth the icing. Neaten the edge and leave to dry. Repeat with a second layer of icing.

To Royal-ice a Square Cake

ROYAL ICING CHART

QUANTITY OF ROYAL ICING	CAKE SIZE
450 g/1 lb/1½ cups	12 cm/5 in square 15 cm/6 in round
675 g/1½ lb/2¼ cups	15 cm/6 in square 18 cm/7 in round
900 g/2 lb/3 cups	18 cm/7 in square 20 cm/8 in round
1.1 kg/2½ lb/3¾ cups	20 cm/8 in square 23 cm/9 in round
1.4 kg/3 lb/4½ cups	23 cm/9 in square 25 cm/10 in round
1.6 kg/3½ lb/5¼ cups	25 cm/10 in square 28 cm/11 in round
1.8 kg/4 lb/6 cups	28 cm/11 in square 30 cm/12 in round
2 kg/4½ lb/6¾ cups	30 cm/12 in square 33 cm/13 in round

Royal Icing Quantity Guide

It is always difficult to estimate how much royal icing will be needed to cover a cake. The quantity varies according to how the icing is applied and to the thickness of layers. The design also has to be taken into consideration – depending upon whether it is just piping, or run-outs and sugar pieces.

Do not attempt to make up large quantities of royal icing in one go. The best method is to make up and use the royal icing in 450 g/1 lb/1½ cup batches (see recipes pages 41 and 42). Each batch of icing will then be fresh and free from any impurities which may occur when larger quantities are made for one cake.

The chart (left) is just a guide to the quantities needed for covering various cakes with two or three thin layers of flat royal icing.

1 Make a quantity of royal icing to soft peak consistency. Cover with clean, damp muslin (cheesecloth). Place the marzipanned cake on a turntable.

2 Using a small palette knife (spatula), spread the icing back and forth over the top of the cake to eliminate any air bubbles before spreading smoothly. Remove the excess icing from the top edges of the cake with the metal palette knife (spatula). Take the cake off the turntable and place on a rigid surface.

3 With the cake directly in front, hold the straight edge comfortably and place it on the top edge at the far side of the cake. Steadily pull the straight edge across the top of the cake in one continuous movement to smooth the icing. If the top is not smooth enough, repeat the movement until it is smooth, or re-spread the top of the cake with icing, neaten the edge and start again. Do not worry about this first layer being perfect.

4 Trim away the excess icing from the top edges of the cake with the clean metal palette knife (spatula) to neaten. Then leave the icing to dry for about two hours or overnight in a warm, dry place.

3

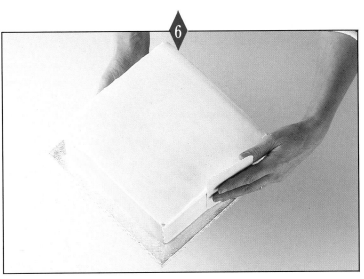

5 Replace the cake on the turntable and using the small palette knife (spatula), smoothly spread one side of the cake with icing to cover evenly. Remove the excess icing from the dry icing on the top edge of the cake and at both corners.

6 Place the cake on a rigid surface and, positioning a side scraper at the far corner of the cake so that it rests on the cakeboard, pull the scraper across the side of the cake in one movement to smooth the icing. If the surface is not satisfactory, repeat the process.

7 Trim away the excess icing from the top edge and the corners of the cake to neaten. Ice the opposite side of the cake in the same way. Neaten the edges and along the cakeboard and leave to dry for at least two hours. Repeat the process to ice the remaining two opposite sides of the cake. Leave to dry overnight before continuing to add further layers of icing.

8 Ice the cake with another two or three thin coats of icing, repeating the method above, until the surface is smooth and flat. For the final coat of icing, to obtain a really smooth finish, use a slightly softer consistency of icing.

To Royal-ice a Square Cakeboard

1 Ensure the icing is completely dry and the cakeboard is free from dry icing. Ice the two opposite sides at a time, smoothing with a side scraper and neaten the edges of the board.
2 Leave to dry. Then repeat to ice the remaining sides and leave to dry. Repeat with a second layer of icing.

Peaked Royal Icing

Royal icing is very versatile and can be smoothed onto a cake to achieve a perfectly flat finish for decorating, or peaked and swirled to give a texture.

To make beautifully even peaks, the icing must be of soft peak consistency.

1 *Spread the top and sides of a marzipanned cake evenly with royal icing. Smooth the top of the cake with a straight edge and the side with a side scraper so the icing is fairly even and completely covers the cake.*

2 *Using a small, clean palette knife (spatula) dip one side of the blade into the bowl of icing. Starting at the base and working to the top edge of the cake, press the palette knife (spatula) with icing onto the iced cake, pulling sharply away to form a peak. Repeat to form about three or four peaks, then re-dip the palette knife (spatula) into the bowl of icing and repeat to make more peaks down the side of the cake, in between the first line, about 10 mm/1/2 in apart. Continue until the side is complete.*

3 *Repeat to peak the top, leaving a smooth area for decorations if desired.*

4 *If the top is to be flat, follow the guide for flat icing the top of a cake and then, when completely dry, spread the sides with soft-peak royal icing and peak as above.*

SUGARPASTE (FONDANT)

Pink-coloured sugarpaste or fondant has been used over a sponge base to create this appealing present-shaped cake for a special birthday.

Sugarpaste (fondant) has become increasingly popular during the last few years. Now celebration cakes are often presented as softly rounded, smooth cakes instead of the sharp, crisp, classical lines of a traditionally iced cake.

There are so many advantages when using this type of icing, the most obvious being that it is quick and easy to make and a treat to use. Being soft and pliable, the icing may be rolled out to any shape and used to cover freshly marzipanned cakes, producing an instant result. Even the least experienced cake decorator can achieve a smooth, glossy, professional finish and – with the minimum amount of decoration – finish the cake.

Although a recipe for a sugarpaste (fondant) is included, there are certainly times when ready-made icing is better or more convenient to use. There are several types of sugarpaste (fondant) or ready-to-roll icing on the market. All have more or less the same ingredients, but are packaged under many different names. Textures may vary and some are certainly better to handle than others. It is a good idea to try a small quantity first to see if it is suitable for the cake you wish to ice.

Sugarpaste (fondant) can be purchased in 225 g/8 oz/½ lb packs from supermarkets and shops, or up to 5 kg/11 lb boxes from cake-icing specialists. Sugarpaste (fondant) is available in white, champagne, pink and many other colours. This is worth considering if you need a large quantity for a wedding cake, as it ensures the colour is even throughout. Kneading food colouring into large quantities of sugarpaste (fondant) is hard work and time-consuming.

Sugarpaste (fondant icing) may be tinted at home in any shade by kneading in a few drops of food colouring until the whole quantity is evenly coloured. It can be used very successfully for covering all types of cakes – for modelling, making sugar flowers, leaves and cut-out sugar decorations.

Sugarpaste
(Fondant Icing)

INGREDIENTS

Makes 575 g/1¼ lb/1¼ lb
- *1 egg white*
- *30 ml/2 tbsp/2 tbsp liquid glucose*
- *10 ml/2 tsp/2 tsp rosewater*
- *450 g/1 lb/1½ cups icing (confectioners) sugar, sieved (sifted)*
- *icing (confectioners) sugar to dust*

1 *Place the egg white, liquid glucose and rosewater into a clean bowl. Mix together to break up the egg white. Add the icing (confectioners) sugar and combine with a wooden spoon until the icing begins to bind together.*

2 *Knead together with the fingers until the mixture forms into a ball.*

3 *Place on a surface lightly dusted with icing (confectioners) sugar and knead until smooth and free from cracks.*

4 *If the icing is too soft to handle and is sticky, knead in some more sieved (sifted) icing (confectioners) sugar until firm and pliable. If the sugarpaste should dry out and become hard, knead in a little boiled water until the icing is soft and pliable.*

STORING

Wrap the icing completely in cling film (plastic wrap), or store in a polythene (polyethylene) bag with all the air excluded.

SUGARPASTE CHART

Cake Tin Sizes	12 cm/5 in Square	15 cm/6 in Square	18 cm/7 in Square	20 cm/8 in Square	23 cm/9 in Square	25 cm/10 in Square	28 cm/11 in Square	30 cm/12 in Square
	15 cm/6 in Round	18 cm/7 in Round	20 cm/8 in Round	23 cm/9 in Round	25 cm/10 in Round	28 cm/11 in Round	30 cm/12 in Round	33 cm/13 in Round
QUANTITIES								
Sugarpaste (fondant)	450 g/ 1 lb	675 g/ 1½ lb	800 g/ 1¾ lb	900 g/ 2 lb	1.1 kg/ 2½ lb	1.5 kg/ 3¼ lb	1.8 kg/ 4 lb	1.9 kg/ 4¼ lb

To Cover Any Shaped Cake with Sugarpaste (Fondant)

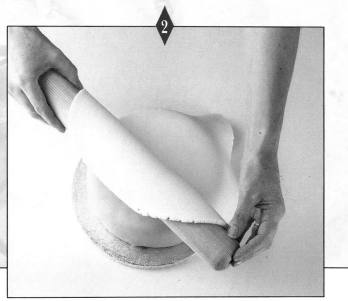

1 Place the marzipanned cake, on the cakeboard, onto a turntable and brush the surface evenly with a little sherry or cooled boiled water. Dust a work surface with sieved (sifted) icing (confectioners) sugar to prevent the sugarpaste from sticking. Roll out the sugarpaste (fondant) to 5 mm/¼ in thickness, using more sieved (sifted) icing (confectioners) sugar if necessary, to the chosen shape of the cake.

2 Trim the sugarpaste (fondant) to 6.5 cm/2½ in larger than the top of the cake, making sure the icing moves freely. Lift the sugarpaste carefully over the top of the cake, supported by a rolling pin. Brush off any excess icing (confectioners) sugar. Unroll the sugarpaste over the cake to cover evenly.

3 Dust your hands with cornflour (cornstarch), and smooth the icing over the top and then down the sides of the cake. Ease the excess icing toward the base, excluding any air bubbles between the surfaces. Trim off excess icing at base of cake using a small knife.

4 Dust your hands with more cornflour (cornstarch), and gently rub the surface of the sugarpaste in circular movements to make it smooth and glossy. Place the cake in a cake box and leave in a warm, dry place to dry the sugarpaste.

5 Knead the trimmings together and seal in cling film (plastic wrap) or a polythene (polyethylene) bag and use to cover the cakeboard, or for decorations.

To Cover Any Shaped Cakeboard with Sugarpaste (Fondant)

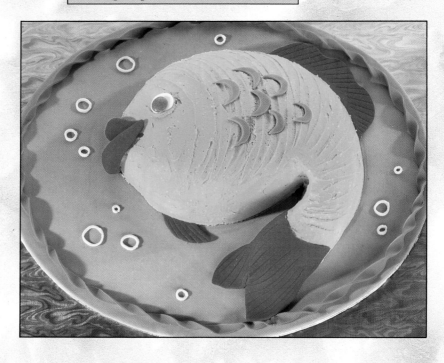

Complete the effect of a novelty or classic cake by continuing the coloured fondant or sugarpaste covering onto the cakeboard.

1 Lightly dust a surface with icing (confectioners) sugar. Tint the sugarpaste (fondant) to the required colour to match the cake. Brush the cakeboard with a little apricot glaze.

2 Roll out the sugarpaste (fondant) to 5 mm/¼ in thickness to the shape of the cakeboard. Ensure the sugarpaste moves freely and lift over the cakeboard. Dust your hands with cornflour (cornstarch), and smooth the surface, trimming off excess icing using a small palette knife (spatula). Keep the blade level with the edge of the board and take care to keep the edge of the sugarpaste (fondant) straight.

3 Leave the iced board in a warm place overnight to dry. Then place the iced cake carefully in position.

PETAL PASTE

Petal paste is used only for making cake decorations. It is exceptionally strong and can be moulded into very fine flowers or cut into individual sugar pieces which dry very quickly. Liquid glucose and gum tragacanth are available from chemists or cake-icing specialists. Petal paste can also be purchased commercially in a powdered form ready to mix, which is very convenient for small quantities but is rather expensive if using large amounts.

INGREDIENTS

Makes 575 g/1¼ lb/1¼ lb
- *10 ml/2 tsp/2 tsp (powdered) gelatine*
- *25 ml/5 tsp/5 tsp cold water*
- *10 ml/2 tsp/2 tsp liquid glucose*
- *10 ml/2 tsp/2 tsp white vegetable fat*
- *450 g/1 lb/3½ cups icing (confectioners) sugar, sieved (sifted)*
- *5 ml/1 tsp/1 tsp gum tragacanth*
- *1 egg white*

Petal paste can be used to make tiny little flowers for a special celebratory or formal birthday cake.

1 *Place the gelatine, water, liquid glucose and white fat in a heatproof bowl over a saucepan of hot water until melted, stirring occasionally. Remove the bowl from the heat.*

2 *Sift the icing (confectioners) sugar and gum tragacanth into a bowl. Make a 'well' in the centre and add the egg white and gelatine mixture. Mix together with a wooden spoon to form a soft paste.*

3 *Knead on a surface dusted with icing (confectioners) sugar until smooth, white and free from cracks.*

4 *Place in a polythene (polyethylene) bag or wrap in cling film (plastic wrap) and seal well to exclude all the air. Leave for two hours before use, then re-knead and use small pieces at a time, leaving the remaining petal paste well sealed.*

FOOD COLOURINGS AND TINTS

Food colourings and tints have changed dramatically over the last few years. At one time food colourings were only available in bottles in a range of primary colours. These liquid colours are still available from most supermarkets and shops and are adequate for tinting icings, frosting, butter icing, marzipan and sugarpaste. With careful blending many other colours and shades can be achieved. Since the colourings are fairly diluted, it is impossible to achieve a richer colour without diluting the consistency of the icing. So for stronger colours, concentrated food colouring pastes produce better results.

PASTE, POWDER AND LIQUID COLOURS

In specialist cake-icing and decorating shops, food colourings are available in a far greater range. Good quality colours appear as pastes, powders and liquids. They are very concentrated and need to be added drop by drop, using a cocktail stick to stir and carefully tint the icing to a delicate shade. An exceptional variety of colours are available so there is no need to blend the colours to obtain the shade of icing you want. Since they are so concentrated, the consistency of the icing is not affected. The colours are also permanent and do not fade.

Remember that food colourings, when added to icings or kneaded into marzipan or sugarpaste, change on standing and dry a deeper or a lighter colour than when first mixed. Colour sample amounts of icing in the daylight and leave them for at least 15 minutes to assess if you have achieved the desired colour. If you are matching icing with fabrics or flowers, allow coloured samples to dry thoroughly before deciding. If several batches of coloured icing are to be made, keep some icing in reserve so the colour can be matched. Always remember that a cake should look edible, so keep the colours to pastel shades – a hint of colour is better than too much.

Celebration cakes may require more subtle shading and tinting. Moulded and cut-out flowers, sugar pieces and cakes' surfaces can now be coloured with 'blossom tints', or painted with 'lustre colours' when the flowers, sugar pieces or icings

are dry. This also gives you an opportunity to add colour at the last minute, and prevents the risk of colours running into the icing when the atmosphere is damp. These products also hold their colour without fading. Such specialist food colours are available only from cake-decorating shops.

FOOD-COLOURING PENS

These pens look like fibre-tip pens but are filled with edible food colourings. They come in a range of primary colours as well as black, brown and purple. Their uses are endless, especially for quickly decorating, writing or applying details to models or sugar pieces.

Use them like a pen to write or draw a design onto dry royal icing run-outs, small sugar plaques or even to mark a design directly onto an iced cake. But these pens are indelible – so make no mistakes!

Marzipan or sugarpaste (fondant) is easily tinted with food colouring; break off small pieces and work in gradually until evenly blended.

USING CHOCOLATE TO DECORATE CAKES

A traditional festive log on a chocolate theme, coated with a deliciously rich chocolate ganache topping and decorated with chocolate flakes.

Chocolate is a very versatile ingredient to work with. Since it is an expensive product, however, it should be used with great care to obtain the best results. Chocolate is sold in many forms – milk, plain and white; in bars, dots, as thick, richly-flavoured spreads, and as powdered cocoa and drinking chocolate.

Choosing Chocolate

There are basically four grades of chocolate for cooking – *couverture*, cooking chocolate, eating or dessert chocolate and chocolate-flavoured cake covering.

COUVERTURE is the finest, most expensive chocolate used for confectionery and special chocolate work. It contains the highest proportion of cocoa butter, which gives the chocolate its fine flavour and texture. When using, it must be tempered to obtain the high gloss and hard texture.

COOKING CHOCOLATE is available in different grades; the quality of the chocolate depends on how much cocoa butter it contains. This affects the flavour, colour and texture. Cooking chocolate is a good all-rounder, is less expensive to buy and ideal for all recipes using cooked chocolate.

EATING OR DESSERT CHOCOLATE has slightly less cocoa butter but a wonderful flavour and refined texture. It is versatile for cooking, but is rather expensive. It is better to select this type of chocolate for special desserts, gateaux or homemade chocolates. When it is melted, it remains quite thick, so it is not suitable for smoothly coated cakes.

CHOCOLATE-FLAVOURED CAKE COVERING actually contains so little cocoa butter that it can no longer be called "chocolate". It has a poorer flavour than the other alternatives and the texture is soft and rather greasy. Points in its favour are that it is easier to use and is less expensive to buy. It is a good all-round cooking product and may be used for all chocolate recipes.

All these grades of chocolate are obtainable as plain (semisweet), milk or white chocolate. The plainer the chocolate, the harder the texture and the stronger the flavour. Milk chocolate is milder and sweeter. White chocolate, containing only cocoa butter and no dark cocoa solids, has no distinctive flavour.

To Melt Chocolate

Break the chocolate into small pieces and place in a large, dry, clean bowl over a saucepan of *hand-hot* water. Ensure that the base of the bowl does not touch the water. Do not beat, but stir it occasionally until it has completely melted; this you cannot hurry and the chocolate temperature should not exceed 38–43°C/100–110°F. Otherwise, when it eventually sets, the surface will be covered with a white fat bloom. Never allow moisture, steam or condensation to come into contact with chocolate or it will become thick

and unstable. Leave the bowl over water during use, unless you require the chocolate to become thicker. Any left-over chocolate can always be re-used so there is no waste.

Chocolate can be melted in a micro-wave set at the lowest setting if time is short, but only if the chocolate is being used to add to other ingredients. For coating and spreading, the chocolate becomes too warm and the surface dries with a streaked appearance.

Coating

1 Stand cakes, candies or biscuits (cookies) on a wire cooling rack, spaced a little apart. Make sure all items to be coated are at room temperature. Place a large piece of greaseproof (wax) paper underneath to catch the excess chocolate. Depending on the size of the piece being coated, use a ladle full of chocolate that will coat the whole item at one coating.

2 Pour the chocolate quickly over, allowing the excess to fall onto the paper below. Tap the cooling rack against the counter surface to level the chocolate. Repeat with another layer after the first one has set, if liked. Return the fallen chocolate from the greaseproof (wax) paper back into the bowl.

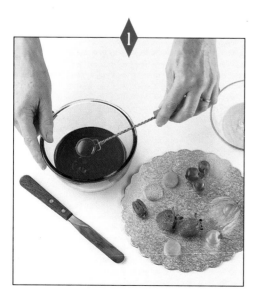

Dipping Fruit

1 *Have everything ready before starting. All items to be dipped should be at room temperature, otherwise the chocolate will set before smoothly coating. Use confectioners' dipping forks or a large dinner fork and have several sheets of baking parchment ready to take the dipped items.*

2 *Place the items individually into the chocolate, turn once with the dipping fork to coat evenly. Lift out with the fork, tap gently on the side of the bowl and allow the excess chocolate to fall. Place on the paper, mark or decorate the top, and leave to set.*

Choose real leaves from flowers, herbs and plants which are small, firm and have well-defined veins.

1 *Melt 125 g/4 oz/4 squares white, plain or milk chocolate. Pick as many fresh leaves as possible, wash them and then dry thoroughly on kitchen paper.*

2 *Using a medium-sized paintbrush, thickly coat the underside of each leaf with melted chocolate, taking care not to paint over the edge of the leaves or the leaf will not peel away from the chocolate.*

3 *Place the leaves to set on baking parchment – chocolate side uppermost – in a cool place. Just before using, peel the real leaves away from their chocolate impressions. The chocolate leaves make exquisite decorations.*

A chocolate cake is always irresistible; not only is the sponge of this cake chocolate, but there is a rich chocolate icing and decorations of chocolate-dipped cherries and chocolate leaves.

Chocolate Curls

1 Melt 125 g/4 oz/4 squares plain, milk or white chocolate. Pour melted chocolate onto a rigid surface such as marble, wood or plastic laminate. Spread evenly backwards and forwards with a palette knife until smooth.
2 When the chocolate has just set, but has not become hard, hold a sharp knife at a 45° angle to the chocolate. Draw the knife across the surface to shave off thin curls from the chocolate.
3 To make larger curls or *caraque*, draw the knife down the whole length or width of the chocolate to form long curls.

4 Make chocolate shavings in the same way, but let the chocolate set a little harder before beginning. Then draw the knife only halfway across the surface to shave off fine flakes.
5 To make tiny curls, use a potato peeler to shave curls off the side of a block of chocolate. This must be at room temperature, unless you are using chocolate-flavoured cake covering, which is just the right texture for curling. Alternatively grate chocolate on a coarse grater.

Chocolate Cut-outs

1 Melt 125 g/4 oz/4 squares milk, plain or white chocolate. Pour the melted chocolate onto baking parchment. Spread as evenly as possible with a palette knife (spatula).

2 Pick up the corners of the paper and drop a few times to level and remove air bubbles from the chocolate.

3 When the chocolate can be touched without sticking to the fingers, place another piece of paper on the top. Turn the whole sheet of chocolate over, then peel off the backing paper. Turn the chocolate sheet over.

4 To cut out shapes: use any shaped cocktail, biscuit (cookie), plain or fluted cutters. Press onto the chocolate, cut out and remove the shapes.

5 To cut out squares or triangles: carefully measure and mark the size of the squares required. Using a fine sharp knife or scalpel and the straight edge of a ruler, cut along the marked lines and remove the shapes. Cut diagonally in half for triangles.

6 Leave in a cool place to set hard before using.

Piped Chocolate

There are easy ways of piping chocolate; one is by using chocolate and hazelnut spread which is the ideal consistency. Place in a greaseproof (wax) paper piping bag fitted with a small star nozzle. With this you can pipe a border of shells, stars or whirls.

Melted chocolate is more difficult to pipe through a metal nozzle, as the coldness of the metal sets the chocolate before you start. Add a few drops of glycerine to the chocolate to thicken it, rather than allowing the chocolate to cool and thicken naturally. Then pipe the chocolate through a nozzle as quickly as possible.

For piping threads or lines of chocolate, use a greaseproof (wax) paper piping bag, snip off the point to the size of the hole required and pipe thin threads of chocolate in straight or zig-zag lines.

TO COLOUR WHITE CHOCOLATE – white chocolate is very versatile and can be coloured. Use oil-based or powdered food colourings, as liquids added to chocolate will cause it to thicken and become unusable.

Piped Chocolate Pieces

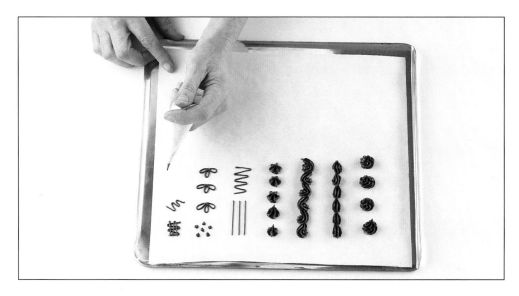

1 Melt 25 g/1 oz/1 square white, plain or milk chocolate. Draw the chosen designs onto a piece of paper. Place greaseproof (wax) paper over the top and secure the corners with tape.

2 Fill a greaseproof (wax) paper piping bag with chocolate. Fold down the top and snip off the end.

3 Pipe fine threads of chocolate following the designs, or pipe free-hand designs. Leave to set, then carefully slide a thin palette knife (spatula) under each piece to release. Use for decorating cakes and gateaux.

Chocolate Run-outs

Choose any simple biscuit- (cookie-) cutter, in shapes such as animals, birds, hearts, flowers, bells, horseshoes, numerals or letters.

1 *Draw or trace the chosen shape several times on a piece of paper to allow for breakages. Place a piece of baking parchment over the top and stick down the edges. Using two greaseproof (wax) paper piping bags, fill each with melted chocolate and fold down the tops. Snip off the point from one piping bag and pipe a thread of chocolate around the edge of the design.*

2 *Cut the end off the remaining piping bag and fill in the run-out with melted chocolate so that it looks rounded. Leave to set.*

3 *Pipe on any details, if necessary, then allow to set hard. Carefully peel off the paper and use as desired.*

MARZIPAN DECORATING IDEAS

Marzipan is smooth, soft and easy to work with – an ideal base for royal icing and sugarpaste (fondant). It may be tinted in various shades with food colourings, or cut into shapes, or moulded into flowers, animals and figures.

Used as a cake covering on its own, it offers colour, texture and flavour without the sweetness of icing or sugarpaste (fondant). Once the cake has been covered in marzipan, it may be decorated very simply by crimping the edges and applying marzipan cut-outs, or moulded leaves, flowers, animals or fruit.

Crimper Designs

These easy and effective designs are obtained by using crimping tools, which are available from most kitchen shops or cake-decorating specialists. They come with a variety of shaped end-pieces – curved lines, scallops, ovals, 'V', hearts, diamonds and zig-zags. To obtain an even crimped design, first practise on a spare piece of freshly-made marzipan. Crimping must always be worked on fresh marzipan.

Cover the cake with marzipan, but do not allow it to dry. Before beginning, dust the crimper with cornflour (cornstarch) to prevent sticking. Place the crimper on the edge of the cake and squeeze firmly to mark the marzipan. Gently release and lift the crimper, taking care it does not spring apart or it will tear the marzipan. Place the crimper end next to the marked section and continue the pattern all around the top of the cake. If desired, use on the base and sides of cakes as well, or make a design across the top.

Cut-out Decorations

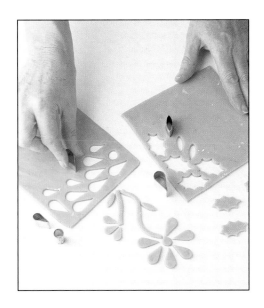

Cut-outs present a simple way of decorating a cake with coloured marzipan.
• Tint several pieces of marzipan with different food colouring, kneading each piece lightly until evenly coloured. Roll out each piece evenly on a surface lightly dusted with sieved (sifted) icing (confectioners) sugar, until about 3 mm/⅛ in thick.
• Using small aspic, cocktail or biscuit (cookie) cutters, cut out a selection of shapes. Arrange them in an attractive design on the cake – either as a border or as a central design – and secure with a coating of apricot glaze.

• Small flower and leaf cutters may be used to make a flower design; an arrangement of stems and other leaves can be cut out from thin strips of coloured marzipan. Mark the veins with a knife and bend the leaves over a piece of dowel until dry.
• Individual cut-out decorations look bright and cheerful on a marzipanned or iced cake. Suggestions for designs include a candle and flame. Cut out a template as a guide for making the coloured marzipan pieces and assemble them on the cake. Other possibilities include book or nursery rhyme characters or scenes from birthday or Christmas cards. Build the shapes by cutting out each piece from different-coloured marzipan.

Rope or Plait

These attractive decorations, made from marzipan, are a quick and simple way to finish the top and base of a cake.

1 To make a rope, simply use two coloured pieces of marzipan rolled into pencil-thin lengths.

2 Join the two ends together and twist to form a rope.

1 To make a plait, use three coloured pieces of marzipan or just one colour and roll them into pencil–thin lengths.

2 Join the ends together and plait the pieces neatly.

Basket Weave

This is fun to do, but takes a little more time and patience. When finished, however, it looks impressive.

1 Work with one or two colours of marzipan. Roll out one piece at a time to 5 mm/¼ in thickness and cut into 5 mm/¼ in wide strips.

2 Arrange several strips in parallel lines a little apart, then weave strips of marzipan in and out to form a basket weave.

Easy Modelling

Marzipan can be moulded like plasticine into many different shapes by copying simple pictures. The decorator can create a still-life of fruits or flowers, or model animals or people. Tint the marzipan to the required shade and mould each piece individually. Assemble the scenes or characters by pressing the pieces together and allow them to dry in a warm place. Use food colouring pens to mark in details.

Simple Flowers

These are also quick and easy to make. Flower cutters can be obtained from icing specialists. Colour the marzipan as required and roll it out thinly. Dip the cutters into cornflour (cornstarch) and cut out the flowers. Bend the petals to give some shape, and mould different-coloured centres or stamens to fit in the centre. Once the blossoms are completely dry, store them in a box until required.

DECORATING WITH SUGARPASTE (FONDANT)

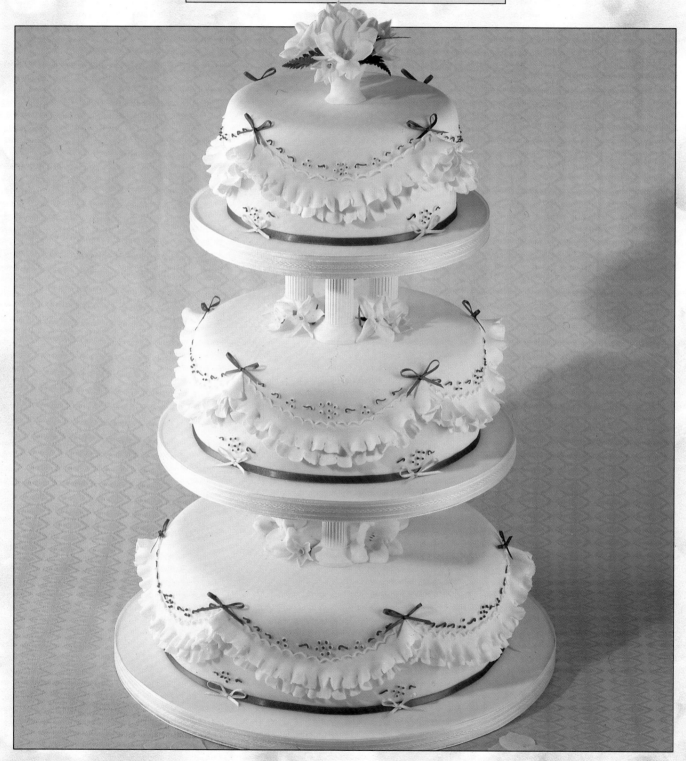

A cake covered in sugarpaste (fondant) looks so different from a royal iced cake – so soft and delicate that it hardly needs decorating; the soft lines and silky finish only demand a dainty finish.

Marbling

Sugarpaste (fondant) lends itself to tinting in all shades, and a very effective way of colouring is to marble the paste. Use it to cover a cake and the cakeboard completely and use the trimmings for cut-out or moulded decorations.

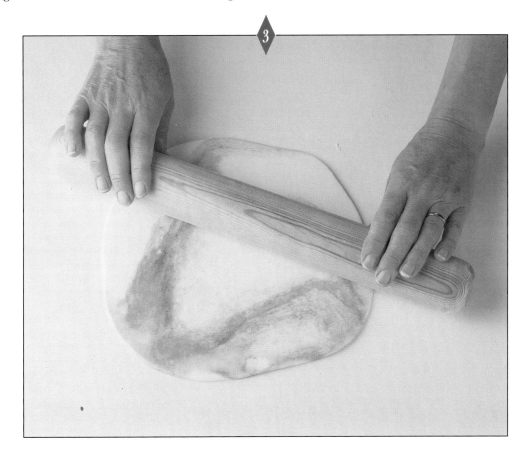

1 *Add a few drops of food colouring in drops over the icing.*

2 *Do not knead the food colouring fully into the icing.*

3 *When it is rolled out, the colour is dispersed in such a way that it gives a marbled appearance to the sugarpaste (fondant).*

Marbling is a wonderful effect easily achieved with sugarpaste or fondant and edible food colourings, as shown with this blue and orange candle-shaped novelty cake.

Frills and Flounces

Frills and flounces are a delicate way of finishing cakes covered smoothly with sugarpaste (fondant). They can be made from ordinary sugarpaste (fondant) but, being soft when worked, the frill has a tendency to drop. To counter this, it is advisable to knead a half teaspoon of gum tragacanth into 225 g/8 oz/½ lb sugarpaste (fondant) 24 hours before use. Alternatively knead one-third petal paste into two-thirds sugarpaste (fondant) until evenly blended. Tint the paste evenly to the colour required.

TO MAKE A FRILL

1 On a surface lightly dusted with cornflour (cornstarch), roll out thinly a small piece of sugarpaste (fondant). Cut out a 7.5 cm/3 in round, using a plain or fluted cutter. Cut out the centre of the round using a 4 cm/1½ in plain cutter. Alternatively, use a special frill cutter, as here.

2 Using the end of a cocktail stick or toothpick sprinkled with cornflour (cornstarch), place on the outer edge of the circle. Roll the cocktail stick along the edge with the fingers until the edge of the icing begins to frill. Move round the edge of the icing until the edge is completely frilled.

3 Cut the ring open with a sharp knife.

4 Gently ease the frill open and attach it to the cake, securing with a line of royal icing or egg white.

Frills made from a blend of sugarpaste (fondant) and petal paste are used to stunning decorative effect on this formal wedding cake.

TO MAKE A FRILLED PLAQUE

1 Colour the sugarpaste (fondant) and roll out thinly. Cut out the shape and size of the plaque required, using an oval or round plain or fluted cutter.

2 Frill the edge following the instructions above.

3 When the plaque is dry, pipe with royal icing to decorate, or use food colouring pens to write on the plaque.

Embossing

This wonderful technique provides an instant way of decorating a cake covered with sugarpaste (fondant). It is similar to crimping in that the cake has to be freshly covered with the icing to work the design.

There are embossing tools in a large range of patterns and designs available from cake-icing specialists. Many other tools may be used to impress a pattern into the sugarpaste (fondant) – spoon handles, tops of icing nozzles, anything small with a defined pattern on it.

Colour may be added by dipping the embossing tool into petal dust before embossing the icing, or by painting part or all the design with food colouring and a fine brush, or with petal dust or food colouring pens, when the sugarpaste (fondant) is dry.

TO EMBOSS A PATTERN

Choose the design you wish to emboss onto the cake. Practise on a small piece of sugarpaste (fondant) to create the design before embarking on the cake.

Ensure the cake is freshly covered in sugarpaste (fondant) and dust the embossing tool with cornflour (cornstarch) or petal dust. Take care to press the embossing tool to the same depth and angle each time to make an even design. Re-dust with petal dust to colour the design or with cornflour (cornstarch) to prevent sticking.

Embossers are a simple way to create a beautiful edging to a formal cake; a horseshoe-shaped embosser is used here for good luck.

Crimping

These quick, easy and effective designs are obtained by the use of crimping tools which are available from most kitchen shops or cake-decorating specialists. They come in different-shaped end pieces, curved lines, scallops, ovals, 'V', hearts, diamonds and zig-zags. To obtain an even crimped design, first practise on a spare piece of sugarpaste (fondant) and always crimp in fresh sugarpaste.

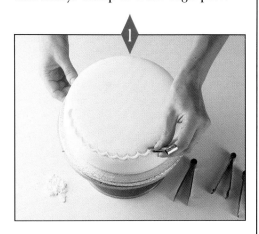

1 Cover the cake with sugarpaste (fondant), but do not allow it to dry. Dust the crimper with cornflour (cornstarch) to prevent sticking. Place the crimper on the edge of the cake and squeeze firmly to mark the sugarpaste (fondant). Gently release and lift the crimper – taking care it does not spring apart or it will tear the sugarpaste (fondant). Place the crimper end next to the patterned paste, squeeze, lift and repeat all around the top of the cake.

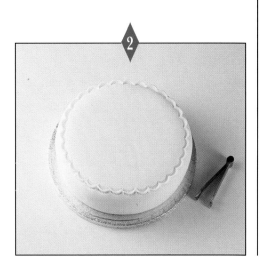

2 Use on the base and sides of cakes as well, if desired, or make a design across the top. Always crimp a cake which has been freshly covered.

Cut-out Decorations

Cut-outs make an instant decoration for an iced cake.

1 Simply colour the sugarpaste (fondant) in the chosen colours, roll out thinly on a surface lightly dusted with icing (confectioners) sugar and cut out small shapes using aspic or cocktail cutters.

2 Lightly press these shapes onto the top and sides of the cake to make a border design and to decorate the sides, securing them with egg white, if necessary. Alternatively, allow the cut-out pieces to dry and store in a box in a warm dry place until required for finishing the cake.

Cut-out sugar pieces in a variety of different shapes have been created to decorate this special birthday cake.

Sugar Pieces and Extensions

Delicate pieces cut out from petal paste need to be fine and strong as generally they are attached to the edges of the cake, extending the design. There are many wonderful shapes to create from petal paste, so work out the design first. Tint the paste a pale shade, or leave it white and dust the pieces with petal dust when they are dry.

Roll out the petal paste in small quantities as it dries quickly. Roll it so thinly that you can almost see through it. Using cutters of varying shapes or a template, cut out the pieces you require. Allow them to dry, then attach them to the cake using royal icing.

Ribbon Insertion

This technique creates the illusion that a single piece of ribbon has been threaded through the sugarpaste (fondant) icing. The design can be straight, diagonal or curved and combined with crimper work or dainty piping. The sugarpaste should feel firm on the surface, but soft underneath. Finish off the ribbon insertion with tiny bows, fine piping or crimping.

Plan the design on paper first, make a template and mark the design accurately onto the cake. Choose the colour and the width of the ribbon required and cut as many pieces as necessary to complete the design. The ribbon pieces should be slightly larger than the spaces, leaving enough room to tuck the ends in.

The technique of ribbon insertion takes a little time to master, but is stunningly effective on special celebratory cakes.

1 *Using a very fine blade or scalpel, cut the slits accurately in the icing following the marked lines.*

2 *Insert one end of the ribbon into the first slit using a pin or fine blade, and tuck the other end of the ribbon into the second slit.*

3 *Leave a space and repeat, until all the slits are filled.*

Cut-out Sugarpaste Flowers

Using flower cutters to make sugarpaste (fondant) flowers must be the simplest way to make a large quantity of flowers quickly. Flower cutters are available from cake-icing specialists and are available in a variety of flower shapes – daisy, rose, simple blossoms, fuchsia and orchids, to name but a few. The most popular shape is the plunger blossom cutter. This comes in three sizes with a plunger which ejects the blossom in the perfect shape.

Plunger Blossom Flowers

Sugarpaste (fondant) or petal paste may be used for these flowers. If you need to wire them onto stems to make sprays, the petal paste is stronger.

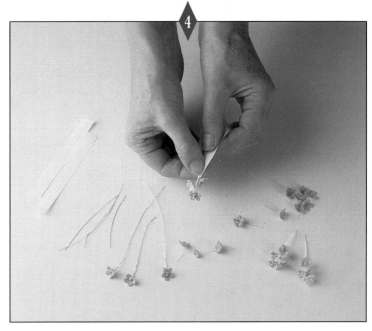

1 *Tint the sugar- or petal paste to the shade you require. Roll out the sugar- or petal paste very thinly on a lightly cornfloured (cornstarched) surface. Cut out the flower shape with a plunger cutter and place on a piece of foam sponge.*

2 *Eject the flower by pressing the plunger into the sponge to bend the paste to shape the flower. Repeat to make small, medium and large blossoms.*

3 *If the flowers are to have a stamen in the centre, make a pin hole in each blossom as it is made. When dry, pipe a bead of royal icing on to the back of the stamen and thread through the sugar blossom to secure.*

4 *When dry, wire these together using fine florist's wire to make sprays.*

PIPING
TECHNIQUES

Simple Piping
*From left to right:
swirls, stars, scrolls,
shells, building up a
trellis design,
filigree work and
beads or dots,
building up a basket
weave design.*

Piping is a skill worth mastering. All that is needed is a good-quality piping bag or a greaseproof (wax) paper piping bag fitted with a straight-sided metal nozzle. This can turn cream, butter icing or royal icing into stars, shells, scrolls or lines to create a simple decoration on a cake.

Although it appears complicated and difficult to do, with practice and following a few guide lines, it is amazing how quickly you will become confident using a piping bag and nozzle. Take every opportunity to pipe instead of spreading or swirling creams, meringue and icing, and you will soon become adept.

To Make a Greaseproof (Wax) Paper Piping Bag

1 Cut out a 38 × 25 cm/15 × 10 in rectangle of greaseproof (wax) paper or baking parchment. Fold diagonally in half to form two triangular shapes, each with a blunt end. Cut along the fold line.

Fold the blunt end of the triangle over into a sharp cone into the centre and hold in position.

2 Then fold the sharp end of the triangle over the cone shape. Hold all the points together at the back of the cone, ensuring the point of the cone is sharp.

3 Turn the points inside the top edge of the cone and crease firmly.

4 Secure with sticky tape or staple if desired.

Piping Equipment and Tips

COMMERCIALLY-MADE PIPING BAGS
These are available ready-made in washable fabric from most cake specialists or kitchen shops. They are especially good to use if you are a beginner as they are easy to handle. Sizes vary from small to large and are ideal for piping cream, buttercream and meringue icing.

PAPER PIPING BAGS
The great advantage of the greaseproof (wax) paper piping bag is that they can be made in advance in various sizes and may be used with or without an icing nozzle. If they are used without a nozzle, simply fill the bag with icing, fold down the top and snip off the end straight to pipe lines, or into a 'V' shape to pipe leaves. After use they can be thrown away. If the icing runs out while using a bag, simply fill a new bag, transferring the icing nozzle first, if necessary. Choose good quality greaseproof (wax) paper or baking parchment for making the bags and follow the instructions on the previous page.

ICING NOZZLES
These are available in a wide variety of shapes and sizes, so it can be quite daunting to know which type to choose. As a beginner, it is advisable to start with a small selection of straight-sided metal piping nozzles as they give a clean, sharp icing result. Begin with two writing nozzles and small, medium and large star nozzles. After mastering the use of these, build up your collection as you try new piping designs. Kept clean and stored carefully in a box or rigid container, the nozzles will never need replacing and are worth the extra expense. Always clean icing nozzles with a nozzle cleaning brush so that the ends do not become bent or damaged.

ICING
Before using any piping equipment, it is essential to have the buttercream or icing at the correct consistency. When a wooden spoon is drawn out of the icing, it should form a fine but sharp point. If the icing is too stiff it will be very difficult to squeeze out of the bag; if too soft, the icing will be difficult to control and the piped shapes will lose their definition.

BASIC PIPING
When piping a celebration cake with royal icing, it is a good idea to practise piping on a board or work surface before starting on the cake. Always ensure the icing is the correct colour and consistency before beginning.

Use a greaseproof (wax) paper piping bag fitted with a straight-sided metal nozzle as this gives a clean, sharp icing pattern. Half-fill the bag with icing – do not be tempted to fill it to the top, as the fuller the icing bag is, the harder it is to squeeze the icing out of the nozzle. This results in aching wrists and hands and poor piping. A good guide is: the smaller the icing nozzle, the less icing you require.

Hold the piping bag comfortably with the nozzle through the first two fingers and thumb, like holding a pencil. Apply the pressure at the top of the bag. The wrists and arms should be relaxed, ready to guide the nozzle.

Simple Piping

Piping is the obvious choice when decorating a cake, but it is easy to be discouraged by attempting too complicated a design. Choose a simple star icing tube and fit it into a greaseproof (wax) paper piping bag to pipe swirls, scrolls and shells.

TO PIPE A SWIRL
Fit the greaseproof (wax) paper piping bag with a star nozzle, half-fill with icing, fold down the top, and squeeze the icing to the end of the nozzle. Place the tip of the icing nozzle just onto the surface of the cake. Press out the icing and pipe a swirl in a circular movement. Stop pressing the bag and pull up sharply to break off the icing. Repeat, piping swirls around the top edge and base of the cake, as desired.

TO PIPE A STAR
Pipe a star shape also from the same nozzle. Hold the bag straight above, at right angles to the surface of the cake. Press the icing out forming a star on the edge of the cake, then pull off sharply to break the icing. Repeat to make a neat border.

TO PIPE SCROLLS
Use the star nozzle and hold the piping bag at an angle so that the nozzle is almost on its side in front of you. Press out the icing onto the top edge of the cake to secure the scroll. Pipe outwards in a circular movement and return the piping nozzle to the edge of the cake. Stop pressing the bag and break off the icing. Repeat again but pipe the icing away from the cake in a circular movement, then return the piping nozzle just to the edge. This is called reverse scrolls, piping scrolls inwards and outwards. For a straight scroll design, pipe the scrolls in one direction only.

TO PIPE SHELLS
Using the star nozzle, hold the piping bag at an angle to the cake so that the nozzle is almost on its side in front of you. Press out some icing and secure to the surface of the cake, pressing gently. Move the nozzle forward, then slowly up, over and down, almost like a rocking movement. Stop pressing and break off the icing by pulling the nozzle towards you. Repeat by piping the icing onto the end of the first shell and continue to make a shell edging.

TO PIPE LINES
Fit a greaseproof (wax) paper bag with a plain writing nozzle; the smaller the hole the finer the lines will be. Fill the bag with icing and pipe a thread of icing, securing the end to the surface of the cake. Continue to pipe the icing just above the surface of the cake, allowing the thread to fall in a straight or curved line. Stop pressing and break off the icing by pulling the nozzle towards you.

To pipe a trellis design, pipe parallel lines of icing in one direction, then over-pipe the lines in the opposite direction. A third series of lines may be piped horizontally across the lattice work to give a better finish.

BASKET WEAVE
Fit a greaseproof (wax) paper piping bag with a ribbon nozzle. Pipe a vertical line from the top of the cake to the bottom. Follow by piping 2 cm/¾ in lines horizontally across the vertical line at 1 cm/½ in intervals. Pipe another vertical line of icing on the edge of the horizontal lines, then pipe short lines of icing in between the spaces across the vertical line to form a basket weave. Repeat all around the cake.

TO PIPE LEAVES

Half-fill a greaseproof (wax) paper piping bag with icing and press the icing to the end of the bag. Cut the end of the piping bag into an inverted 'V'. Place the tip on the surface of the cake. Press out the icing to form a leaf shape, then sharply break off the icing. Repeat to make a pretty border, to add to stems or flowers, or to make a design.

FILIGREE OR CORNELLI WORK

Half-fill a greaseproof (wax) paper piping bag, fitted with a plain writing nozzle, with icing. Hold the icing bag like a pen between the thumb and forefinger. Pipe a continuous thread of icing into 'W' and 'M' shapes, keeping the flow of icing constant, work in all directions, not in lines.

You will need larger nozzles to pipe butter icing and fresh cream. They are, however, available in a wide range of designs for piping swirls, stars, shells and scrolls as described here.

TO PIPE BEADS OR DOTS

To pipe beads of icing is relatively simple, but the icing must be of a softer consistency than usual. This prevents the bead from ending in a sharp point.

Fit a greaseproof (wax) paper piping bag with a No. 3 plain nozzle. Half-fill with icing and fold down the top. Press the icing out just above the surface of the cake to form a rounded bulb. Pull upwards sharply to break off the icing. Repeat to make a border of nicely rounded beads.

Piped Sugar Pieces

Piped sugar pieces are really very useful decorations to make. They can be piped in advance and, when dry, stored in boxes between layers of tissue paper. Any simple shape may be copied by piping royal icing, made with double-strength egg albumen without the addition of glycerine. Use a No. 0 or 1 fine plain writing nozzle.

1 *Draw the chosen design several times on a piece of paper. Cover with a piece of run-out silk or baking parchment and secure at each corner with tape. Fit a greaseproof (waxed) paper piping bag with a No. 1 plain writing nozzle and quarter-fill with royal icing. Fold down the top. Pipe a continuous thread of icing to follow the design showing through the overlay.*

2 *Repeat, moving the base paper underneath the run-out silk or baking parchment to pipe more designs.*

71

Icing Run-outs

Icing run-outs are one of the most exacting forms of cake decoration. They can be made in any shape or form by simply tracing over a chosen design or pattern. Small run-outs can be made in advance and kept between layers of greaseproof (wax) paper in a box stored in a dry place. Larger run-outs and collars are more difficult to store as they may warp during storage. They are better made when needed, dried completely, and applied directly to the cake.

Since run-outs are made from royal icing, they are very fragile. It is wise to choose a small solid shape at first, and make more than required to allow for breakages. When you are confident in making the smaller solid shapes, practise making finer pieces, figures and scenes.

ROYAL ICING

This is a demanding medium. The consistency and texture of the icing must be just right, or the run-outs will be difficult to handle. Use double-strength dried egg albumen, or egg whites with no additives such as glycerine or lemon juice. When the spoon is lifted, a soft peak should form which will bend at the tip. This is the consistency required for piping the outline of the run-outs.

Icing to fill in the run-out must be soft enough to flow with the help of a paintbrush, but hold its shape until tapped, when it becomes smooth. Dilute the royal icing with reconstituted double-strength egg albumen and test a little on a flat surface to determine the consistency. Leave the icing to stand overnight if possible, covered with damp muslin (cheesecloth), allowing any air bubbles to come to the surface. Stir until the air bubbles have dispersed before using.

To Make an Icing Run-out

Draw or trace the chosen design several times on a piece of paper, spaced well apart. Cover the design with a piece of perspex or glass and cover with a sheet of run-out silk or fine waxed paper. Secure the paper to a flat surface with sticky tape or beads of icing.

Fit a greaseproof (wax) paper piping bag with a No. 1 writing nozzle. Half-fill with icing of a slightly stiffer consistency to pipe the outline. Fill a second piping bag with soft icing.

1 With the first bag, fitted with the writing nozzle, pipe carefully over the outline of the design. Use a continuous thread of icing or one with as few breaks as possible. Begin by squeezing out a little icing at the least focal point of the run-out to secure the icing thread to the paper. Lift the thread of icing just above the surface and squeeze the bag, gently following the outline of the tracing, and allow the thread to fall on the marked line around the shape of the run-out. Stop squeezing to prevent the icing thread from running on, and join the icing at the point where it started.

2 Snip the pointed end off the bag half-filled with soft icing and fill in the run-out. Start by piping around the inside edge to keep the outline soft, with less chance of breaking. Work towards the centre, filling the shape so that the icing looks rounded and over-filled and not flat, as the icing shrinks as it sets.

Use a fine paintbrush or cocktail stick to brush over the run-out, ensuring the area is completely filled, and that the icing is smooth and rounded. Gently tap the perspex so that any air bubbles rise to the surface; burst any with a pin. Lift the perspex or glass off the design, move and repeat the design.

3 If the run-out is large, leave it in position to dry. For smaller run-outs, carefully release from the run-out silk or fine waxed paper and transfer to a flat board and leave to dry. Cover the drawing design with more run-out silk or waxed paper and repeat to make as many run-outs as required.

Leave the run-outs under a spotlight, if possible, to dry the surface quickly. Otherwise place in a warm, dry place

overnight until they have set hard. The more quickly they dry, the glossier the run-outs will be. Pipe any detail onto the run-out at this stage and allow to dry. Carefully peel off the paper from the run-out and store the icing decoration in a box between layers of greaseproof (wax) paper until required. Arrange the run-outs on top of the cake and secure with small beads or a line of royal icing.

Simple Flowers Piped With a Petal Nozzle

Many simple flowers can be piped with the aid of a petal nozzle. The size of the nozzles are small, medium and large, and right- and left-handed. Fit the nozzle in a greaseproof (wax) paper piping bag and half-fill with royal icing; fold down the top. Practise several times to get the feel of the nozzle, and it is easier to use an icing nail or piping turntable.

ROSE
Secure a piece of greaseproof (wax) paper to the piping turntable with a bead of icing. Using a petal nozzle, pipe the cone-shaped centre on to the paper and, turning the turntable at the same time, keep the nozzle upright with the thick end of the nozzle at the base.

Pipe a petal two-thirds of the way round the centre cone, turning the turntable at the same time as piping the petal. Repeat to pipe another three petals, at the same time keeping the top of the petal curled outwards.

To pipe the final petals, hold the piping bag at an angle instead of upright. These last petals should be almost flat, to make the rose look in full bloom.

TO PIPE A ROSEBUD
Pipe the centre cone and three petals close together.

DAISY
Use the icing turntable and a square of greaseproof (wax) paper secured with a bead of icing. Hold the petal nozzle on the side so it is flat. Pipe a tiny petal shape in a flat loop, at the same time turning the turntable. Continue to pipe about 12 tiny petals in a circle. Using yellow icing, pipe several small beads to fill the centre.

PANSY
Pipe the pansy petals like the daisy, using white, yellow or purple icing. Holding the petal nozzle flat, pipe the petal shape in a large rounded loop while turning the turntable. Pipe another two petals, one on each side, broad side to the centre. Pipe the fourth petal to join up the circle. Pipe the last petal the opposite way round. Pipe yellow threads of icing in the centre. Using food colouring pens, colour in the markings of the pansy.

FORGET-ME-NOTS
Half-fill the piping bag with white royal icing on the broad side of the nozzle, and pale blue royal icing on the narrow side. Fold down the top and press the icing to the end of the nozzle.

Hold the petal nozzle almost flat to the turntable, with the broad side of the nozzle towards the centre. Pipe a rounded petal, at the same time revolving the turntable. Pipe another four petals, each overlapping the first, to form a circle. Pipe a bead of yellow icing in the centre of the bi-coloured petals.

APPLE BLOSSOM
Pipe these as for forget-me-nots but substitute pale pink for half the icing and white for the remaining icing. Finish with piped green dots in the centre.

A selection of piped flowers in a variety of types, sizes and shades, showing the versatility of this decorative technique.

NARCISSUS
Pipe the white narcissus petals in the same manner as the forget-me-nots, but move the nozzle out and in again to form a long shaped petal. Pipe the first three petals apart, then pipe the remaining three petals in between. Pipe a coil of yellow icing from a No. 1 plain writing nozzle to form the centre. Paint the top with orange food colouring if you wish a bolder variety.

Flowers Piped from a Greaseproof (Wax) Paper Piping Bag without a Nozzle

There are many simple flower forms which can be piped from a greaseproof (wax) paper piping bag by snipping an inverted 'V' from the end of the bag. The piped icing forms into tiny leaf or petal shapes and when grouped into circles or clusters, they form simple flower shapes. Colour the icing to suit the cake design, and give the blossoms contrasting centres.

TO PIPE FLOWER FORMS
Tint the icing to the colour you require. Half-fill a greaseproof (wax) paper piping bag, fold down the top and press the icing to the point. Flatten the point with your fingers and cut an inverted 'V' with a pair of sharp scissors.

Secure a square of greaseproof (wax) paper to the piping turntable with an icing bead. Pipe a circle of petals. Add a double row of petals if desired. Using yellow or white icing, pipe beads or coils of icing into the centre of each flower.

SIMPLE DECORATIONS

Everyday ingredients, used with imagination and flair, are very useful for decorating cakes. Most require very little time. It is particularly rewarding to add the finishing touches to simple cakes, turning them into something a little more special. The ingredients and ideas that follow may inspire you to create your own designs.

A selection of simple and edible cake decorations: glacé and crystallized fruits, citrus fruits, nuts, sweets (candies) and ready purchased decorations.

Icing (Confectioners) Sugar

This is an ingredient which, when used carefully, can transform the appearance of a cake. Simply dusting the surface with the sugar makes a sponge cake more appealing.

Try placing a patterned doiley on top of a cake, or arranging 1 cm/½ in strips of paper in lines or a lattice pattern on top of the cake; then dredge thickly with the icing (confectioners) sugar. Carefully remove the doiley or paper strips, revealing the pattern in sugar. It looks most effective when used on a chocolate or coffee cake where there is a strong colour contrast.

Cocoa and Coffee

These may be used in a similar way to obtain a strong contrast on a light-coloured cake, such as white icing or cream-finished gateaux. Mix cocoa or coffee with a little icing (confectioners) sugar and use to dredge thickly to transfer the doiley or paper-lattice design.

A skewer, cocktail stick or toothpick dipped into cocoa or coffee, then pressed onto the surface of an iced cake will also produce a decorative design.

Citrus Fruits

These fruits are very versatile and offer effective edible decorations from both the fruit and the rind.

Cut oranges, lemons or limes into wedges, segments or round slices, with or without the rind, and use to decorate cakes or gateaux.

The rind, when cut into thin strips using a zester or *canelle* cutter, can transform the appearance of a simply-iced cake. Use to make a fine shred border, or arrange on top of cream whirls. To make decorative stars, crescents or diamonds, cut thin strips of lemon, orange or lime rind from the fruit, taking care not to include the white pith. Using tiny aspic or cocktail cutters, cut out the desired shapes. Arrange them on glacé- or butter-iced cakes as a continuous border design, perhaps using the same shape but different-coloured rinds, or cut the rind to form flowers, stems and leaves.

Glacé or Crystallized Fruits

Preserved fruits are always a good stand-by and can give a charming finish to a cake. Angelica can be cut into stems, leaves and diamond shapes. Glacé cherries in green, red or yellow can be used whole, cut into halves or thin wedges and arranged as petal shapes to make flowers, or cut into slices and used in a border design. Crystallized fruit, although expensive, makes a colourful finish to a rich or plain cake. Slice the fruit thinly and arrange the colourful slices in abstract designs over the top of the cake. Brush with apricot glaze to give a glossy finish.

Nuts

These are also versatile as a quick decoration. Whole assorted nuts arranged over the top of a cake and glazed with honey or sugar syrup look particularly tempting. Nuts dipped in caramel are also attractive, and chopped nuts are invaluable for coating the sides of iced cakes or creamy gateaux.

Commercially-made Decorations

Always have a selection of these to use as standby decorations. Applied with care, they make a very pretty finish to a simple cake. Sugar flowers, jelly diamonds, crystallized flower petals, and marzipan fruits all make eye-catching toppings on swirls of icing, or pressed on to make a border pattern. Coloured almonds, dragées, yellow mimosa balls, hundreds and thousands (multicoloured titbits), chocolate chips and coloured sugar strands make quick and colourful instant coatings, toppings and designs.

Sweets (Candies)

Always a favourite for children's cakes, these decorations come in all shapes, colours and sizes. White or dark chocolate buttons are classic options, while yogurt-coated nuts and raisins offer a healthy alternative. Jelly beans, chocolate beans and liquorice sweets can all be used for simple finishes and decorations on party, novelty or simple cakes.

Flowers

Tiny fresh flowers positioned at the last minute look delectable. Even better are sugar-frosted flowers preserved by the egg white and sugar; they will last for several weeks once they are completely dry. Teamed with fine ribbons tied into tiny bows, they impart a romantic, feminine appeal.

A more practical alternative is offered by silk or artificial flowers which are available from cake-icing specialists or from department stores. Chosen carefully for colour and size, they make instant, re-usable decorations on many cakes.

Use ribbons to decorate cakeboard edges, or make loops and bows for cake tops and flower sprays. Fresh flowers can be used as they are or sugar-frosted or choose silk or paper flowers.

Ribbons

Invaluable for decorating cakes, it is the one non-edible decoration which simply transforms the plainest cake into something quite special. There are over 100 colours available, ranging in width from 1 mm–5 cm/¹⁄₁₆–2 in with plain and fancy edges. Choose double-faced polyester satin ribbons and use to make loops, bows for cakes and flower sprays, and circle around the sides of cakes. Band the cakeboards with ribbons to match the cake design and colour. The best selection of ribbons are from cake-icing and decorating suppliers, who also make matching ribbon bows.

Sugar-frosted Flowers and Leaves

Choose fresh, simple, small flowers with fairly flat petals such as violets, primroses, tiny daffodils, freesias, fuchsias. If possible, pick or buy the flowers just before you need to frost them and ensure they are young blooms. You will need 1 egg white, lightly beaten and caster (superfine) sugar.

1 Dry the flowers with kitchen paper and leave a small stem intact, if possible. Using a fine paintbrush, paint both sides of the flower petals and stem with egg white.

2 Spoon the sugar over the flower petals to coat evenly on both sides, and carefully shake to remove excess sugar.

3 Place in a warm place on a wire rack covered with kitchen paper until dry. To help keep their shape, some flowers are better dried with the stems upwards and the petals flat on the paper. Sugar-frost the leaves in the same way, choosing firm leaves with distinctive shapes.

4 When completely dry, store the flowers in a box between layers of kitchen paper, taking care not to damage them. Use to decorate all types of cakes.

Sugar-frosted Fruits

Choose small, fresh fruits in peak condition such as grapes, cherries, strawberries, lychees, Cape gooseberries and kumquats. You will need 1 egg white, lightly beaten and caster (superfine) sugar.

1 Wipe the fruit with kitchen paper so that the surface is completely dry.
2 Brush each piece of fruit evenly with egg white. Spoon the sugar over the fruit to cover evenly. Leave to dry on kitchen paper.
3 Arrange in a fruit bowl, place in separate paper cases to serve as petit fours, or keep to decorate cakes.

Making Basic Caramel

Care must be taken when making caramel. The sugar syrup is boiled at a very high temperature, turning the syrup a golden amber colour. It has endless uses – for dipping fruits and nuts, crushing for cake coating, or drizzling into shapes for decorating. You will need 150 ml/¼ pt/⅔ cup water and 175 g/6 oz/¾ cup caster (superfine) sugar.

1 Place the water in a saucepan. Bring to the boil, remove the saucepan from the heat and stir in the sugar. Heat gently until the sugar has completely dissolved. Remove the spoon.
2 Bring the syrup to the boil, boil rapidly for several minutes until the bubbles begin to subside and the syrup begins to turn a pale golden brown. Watch carefully at this stage, as the syrup continues to darken when it is taken off the heat.
3 The caramel is ideal for using when it has become a rich golden brown. Allow the bubbles to subside, then use as required.

Caramel Coating

Pour hot caramel thinly over a baking sheet lined with a piece of lightly-oiled foil. Leave until cold, then crush the hardened candy with a rolling pin. Use to coat the sides of an iced cake or gateau.

Making praline and abstract shapes in caramel.

Abstract Caramel Designs

Using a teaspoon, drizzle threads of caramel onto a piece of lightly-oiled foil to make small abstract shapes. If the caramel in the pan begins to set, warm the saucepan over a gentle heat until it begins to melt. When the shapes are set on the foil, lift them off carefully and use for decorations.

To Make Praline

1 Scatter 75 g/3 oz/¾ cup of almonds or hazelnuts over a baking tray and toast at 200°C/400°F/Gas mark 6 until golden brown.
2 Line a board with foil and brush lightly with oil. Make the caramel according to the recipe above. When the bubbles subside, add the warm toasted nuts to the pan. Carefully shake the pan to mix well, then pour the mixture thinly over the oiled foil. Leave to cool.
3 Peel off the foil and crush the caramel and nuts finely with a rolling pin to make a coarse praline. Alternatively place in a food processor and process until finely ground.

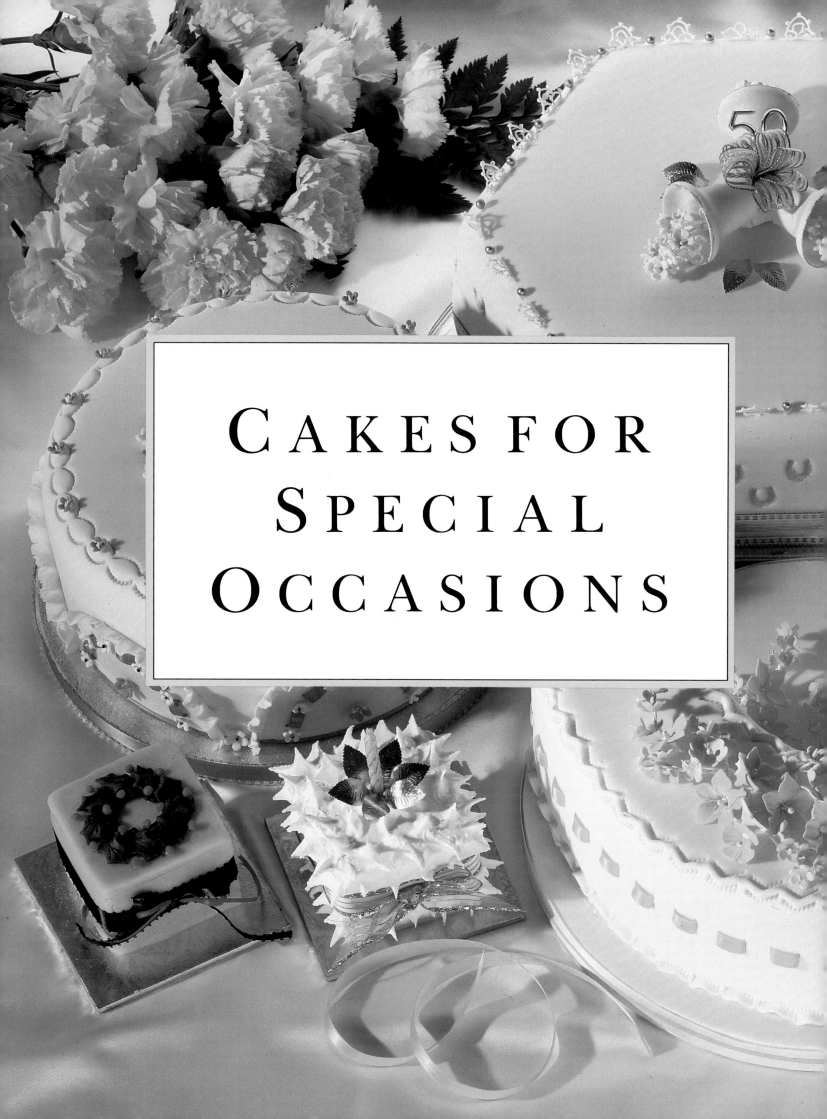

CAKES FOR SPECIAL OCCASIONS

INTRODUCTION

Cakes made for special occasions and special people warrant a lot of care and attention to detail. So take some time to plan. How many people are you hoping to serve? Is the cake for children or adults, a man or a woman? The answers to these questions will determine the choice of base (fruit or sponge), the cake size and shape, the choice of icing and the colour scheme.

Here you will find a wealth of ideas for cakes for all occasions, using many different decorating techniques, icings and colour schemes. There is a classic royal-iced

and an American-style butter-iced wedding cake, and a lovely fresh summer wedding cake made of tiered meringue rings, cream and soft fruits; there is a range of cakes for seasonal festivities, including fun miniature Christmas gift cakes and a traditional Easter simnel cake; and there are birthday, anniversary, christening and retirement cakes in all shapes and designs to suit everyone. Follow the step-by-step guides, but use your own ideas too and change the colours, decorations and ribbon trims, as wished, to create your own individual designs tailored to your particular special occasions.

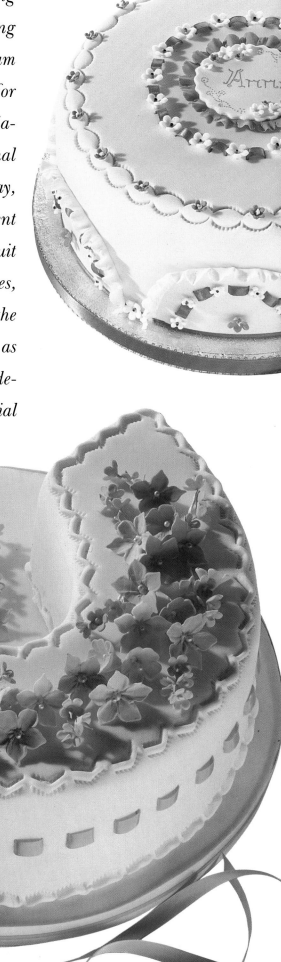

CHOCOLATE LEAF WEDDING CAKE

Lovers of chocolate – this cake has been designed for you: a moist chocolate Madeira cake is covered with marzipan and chocolate-flavoured sugarpaste (fondant). The decorations consist of pretty coral-coloured sugar flowers and assorted chocolate leaves.

INGREDIENTS

Serves 130
- 30 × 25 cm/12 × 10 in oval, deep, chocolate-flavoured Madeira cake
- 25 × 20 cm/10 × 8 in oval, deep, chocolate-flavoured Madeira cake
- 120 ml/4 fl oz/¹/₂ cup apricot glaze
- 2.75 kg/6 lb/6 lb homemade or commercial white marzipan
- 3.25 kg/7 lb/7 lb sugarpaste (fondant)
- 450 g/1 lb/4 cups cocoa powder
- 350 g/12 oz/³/₄ lb petal paste
- yellow and pink food colouring
- 175 g/6 oz/1 cup plain chocolate chips, melted
- 125 g/4 oz/³/₄ cup white chocolate chips, melted
- 125 g/4 oz/³/₄ cup milk chocolate chips, melted
- 30 ml/2 tbsp/2 tbsp royal icing

DECORATION

- 3 m/3 yd × 2.5 cm/1 in wide peach ribbon
- 4 m/4 yd × 1 cm/¹/₂ in wide peach ribbon
- 5 m/5 yd × 5 mm/¹/₄ in wide coral ribbon
- 1 m/1 yd × 5 mm/¹/₄ in wide light coral ribbon

MATERIALS AND EQUIPMENT

- 35 × 30 cm/14 × 12 in oval silver cakeboard
- 25 × 20 cm/10 × 8 in thin oval silver cakeboard
- flower cutter
- blossom plunger cutter
- 30 peach pearl stamens
- flower tape and wire
- greaseproof (wax) paper piping bag
- No. 1 plain writing nozzle

TO MAKE THE CAKE

For a 30 × 25 cm/12 × 10 in and a 25 × 20 cm/10 × 8 oval cake, use quantities of cake mix suitable for a 30 cm/12 in and a 25 cm/10 in round cake. Bake the cakes one at a time and store for up to one week before icing.

1 To level the cakes, cut a slice off the top. Invert the cakes on to their cakeboards and brush with apricot glaze. Cover each cake with marzipan.

2 Divide the sugarpaste (fondant) into three pieces. Knead 125 g/4 oz/¹/₂ cup cocoa powder into each piece until the sugarpaste is evenly-coloured, then knead all the pieces together. Cover the larger cake using half the sugarpaste (fondant), so there is plenty of icing to manipulate, dusting the surface with plenty of cocoa powder and using cocoa powder on your hands to smooth the surface. Repeat to cover the smaller cake and the large cakeboard. Store in boxes in a warm, dry place for up to one week.

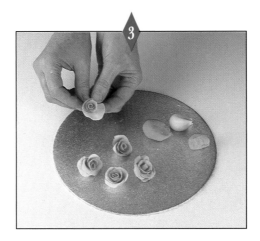

3 To make the sugar flowers, divide the petal paste into three pieces. Using the yellow and pink food colourings, tint one piece pale, one piece medium and one piece dark coral. Make five roses, starting with dark centres and working out to pale petals.

4 Make 25 cut-out flowers of varying shades of coral paste and add stamens.

5 Make 40 plunger blossom flower sprays with the remaining stamens, wire and tape. Leave all the flowers to dry overnight and store in boxes in a warm, dry place. Using a piece of petal paste, press 30 blossom sprays in position to make an arrangement for the top.

6 To make the chocolate leaves, collect a variety of different-shaped leaves (rose, bay, camelia, fruit) and coat 30 with plain chocolate, 15 with white chocolate and 15 with milk chocolate. Store in a cool place until required, then peel off the leaves and keep the chocolate leaves separate on kitchen paper.

7 The day before the wedding, place the royal icing in a greaseproof (wax) paper piping bag fitted with a No. 1 plain writing nozzle. Measure and fit the wide peach ribbon around the larger cakeboard, securing it at the back with a pin. Fit the 1 cm/½ in wide peach ribbon around the base of the larger cake. Fix the fine coral ribbon over the top, and secure with a bead of royal icing. Arrange the cut-out flowers, roses and assorted chocolate leaves around the base of the cake, securing with royal icing.

8 Measure and fit the remaining 1 cm/ ½ in wide ribbon around the base of the small cake with the coral ribbons over the top, securing with royal icing. Carefully place the cake in position on top of the larger cake so that the backs of the cakes are level.

9 Arrange the sprays of blossom, cut-out flowers and chocolate leaves at intervals around the base of the small cake on the edge of the larger cake. Secure all decorations with royal icing. Carefully remove the top cake. Place the sugar flower arrangement onto the top of the cake and arrange the chocolate leaves so they come over the edge. Secure each leaf with royal icing. Using the remaining fine ribbon and fine wire, make some ribbon loops with tails. Press these into the arrangement. Re-box the cakes until the next day, then re-assemble just before the reception.

CLASSIC WEDDING CAKE

The sharp, classical lines of this royal-iced wedding cake give it a very regal appearance. This traditional all-white cake has just a hint of peach in the ribbon decoration.

INGREDIENTS	DECORATION	MATERIALS AND EQUIPMENT
Serves 100	• *4 m/4 yd × 2.5 cm/1 in wide white ribbon*	• *35 cm/14 in square silver cakeboard*
• *30 cm/12 in square rich fruit cake*	• *2 m/2 yd × 2 cm/³⁄4 in wide peach ribbon*	• *a sheet of perspex or glass*
• *75 ml/5 tbsp/5 tbsp apricot glaze*	• *1 m/1 yd × 5 mm/¹⁄4 in wide peach ribbon*	• *run-out silk or greaseproof (wax) paper*
• *1.8 kg/4 lb/4 lb homemade or commercial white marzipan*	• *fresh 'paper white' flowers*	• *greaseproof (wax) paper piping bags*
• *1.8 kg/4 lb/6 cups royal icing (for covering)*		• *No. 3 plain writing nozzle and medium star nozzle*
• *900 g/2 lb/3 cups royal icing made with double-strength egg albumen (for run-outs)*		• *tiny vase*

1 Brush the fruit cake with apricot glaze and cover with marzipan. Place the cake on the cakeboard.

2 Make the royal icing for covering the cake. Flat ice the top and sides of the cake with three or four smooth layers of royal icing. Leave the cake to dry overnight, then ice the cakeboard. Place in a cake box and store in a warm, dry place. Reserve the remaining royal icing for decoration.

3 Make up the royal icing for the run-outs, unless you have plenty left over from the flat icing, in which case add double-strength egg albumen to dilute it. Trace over the templates provided, cover with a piece of perspex or glass, and cover with run-out silk or greaseproof (wax) paper. Tape down to secure. As each run-out is piped and filled in, move the perspex or glass along to reveal the template, and repeat the procedure.

4 Make six corner pieces and six side pieces, allowing for breakage. Pipe in the details when the pieces are dry.

5 Measure and fit the white ribbon around the cakeboard and sides of the cake, securing with a bead of royal icing. Fit the wide peach ribbon over the top of each white band, securing with icing. Make some loops and bows from thin peach ribbon for the top arrangement.

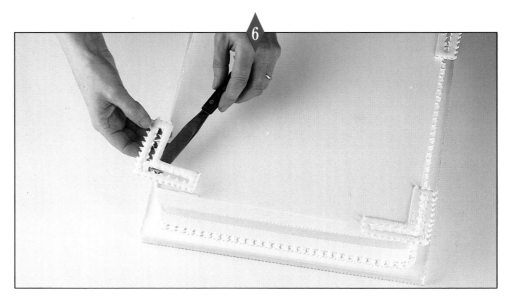

6 Carefully release the run-out pieces and half-fill a greaseproof (wax) paper piping bag fitted with a No. 3 plain writing nozzle with the reserved royal icing. Pipe a line of icing at one corner. Carefully place a corner run-out in position; press very gently to make sure the run-out is secure. Repeat to attach all the corner pieces and the side pieces.

7 Pipe a bead edging in between the run-outs on the top edge of the cake. Using a medium-sized star nozzle, pipe a star edging around the base of the cake. Make a pretty arrangement of fresh flowers in a tiny vase to go on top of the cake, and decorate with ribbons and bows.

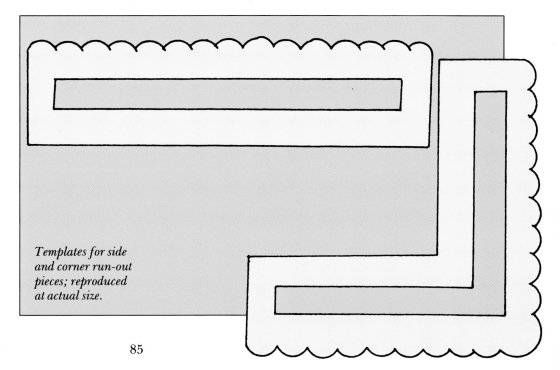

Templates for side and corner run-out pieces; reproduced at actual size.

MIDSUMMER WEDDING CAKE

This lovely meringue wedding cake is fresh and light, and is ideal for a summer wedding when all the soft fruits are in abundance.

INGREDIENTS

Serves 40
- 8 egg whites
- 5 ml/1 tsp/1 tsp cream of tartar
- 500 g/1 lb 2 oz/2¼ cups caster (superfine) sugar
- 550 ml/1 pt/2½ cups double (heavy) cream
- 300 ml/½ pt/1¼ cups whipping cream
- 350 g/12 oz/2 cups redcurrants
- 350 g/12 oz/2 cups white currants
- 350 g/12 oz/2 cups raspberries
- 350 g/12 oz/2 cups fraises des bois or tiny strawberries
- 350 g/12 oz/2 cups blueberries
- 30 ml/2 tbsp/2 tbsp Kirsch

DECORATION

- 8 tiny pink rosebuds
- small fresh strawberry leaves
- 1½ m/1½ yd × 2 cm/¾ in wide white ribbon
- 1½ m/1½ yd × 1 cm/½ in wide dark pink ribbon
- 1½ m/1½ yd × 5 mm/¼ in wide plain dark pink ribbon
- 1½ m/1½ yd × 5 mm/¼ in wide plain light pink ribbon

MATERIALS AND EQUIPMENT

- 30 cm/12 in round silver cakeboard
- 4 large baking sheets
- baking parchment
- nylon piping bags
- 1 cm/½ in plain and small star gateau nozzles

1 Preheat the oven to the lowest setting 110°C/220°F/Gas ¼. Line two large baking sheets with non-stick baking parchment. Draw a 25 cm/10 in circle on one sheet and 18 cm/7 in and 15 cm/6 in circles on the remaining sheet of paper. Invert the sheets of paper.

2 To make the meringue, whisk 4 egg whites and 2.5 ml/½ tsp/½ tsp cream of tartar in a large clean bowl until stiff. Very gradually whisk in 250 g/9 oz/1 good cup of caster (superfine) sugar, whisking really well between each addition, until the meringue stands up in stiff peaks. Place the meringue in a large nylon piping bag fitted with a 1 cm/½ in plain gateau nozzle.

3 Pipe a continuous circle of meringue following the marked lines on each circle. Then pipe a coil from the centre to the edge to fill in each round. Pipe leftover meringue into 5 small rounds in between the circles. Bake in the oven for 2–3 hours until the meringue is dry and the paper peels away easily from the base.

4 Meanwhile line two more baking sheets with baking parchment and draw a 23 cm/9 in, a 10 cm/4 in and a 5 cm/2 in circle onto one sheet of paper and a 20 cm/8 in, a 13 cm/5 in and a 7.5 cm/3 in circle on the remaining sheet of paper. Invert the two papers.

5 Using the remaining egg whites, cream of tartar and sugar, make the meringue circles following the above instructions. When all the meringues are cold, cut around the paper to separate them. Store them in airtight containers on the paper in a warm, dry place until required.

6 Measure and fit the white and the wide pink ribbons around the edge of the cakeboard, securing with a pin.

7 Place the creams into a bowl and whip until just thick; reserve one-third for piping. Whisk the remaining cream until slightly thicker.

8 Reserve several stems of red and white currants for decoration and remove the stems and hulls from the remaining fruits. Mix all the fruits together in a large bowl and sprinkle with Kirsch. Add the fruit to the cream and fold in until well blended. Place one-third of the reserved cream in a nylon piping bag fitted with a small star gateau nozzle.

9 Place the largest circle of meringue on the cakeboard and spread evenly with the cream and fruit mixture to give about a 2 cm/³/4 in deep layer. Top with the next size of meringue round and spread with more of the filling. Cover with the next meringue layer and repeat to use all the layers.

10 Pipe small stars of cream in between the layers to seal in the filling and to decorate the joins. Pipe a swirl of cream on the top and arrange 4 tiny meringue rounds in a circle and one on the top.

11 Press individual redcurrants or other fruits if you prefer into alternate cream stars and 4 tiny rosebuds around the top. Measure and fit 3 dark and 3 light ribbon lengths from the top of the cake to the board. Decorate the board with the reserved currants, leaves and rosebuds. Keep in a cold place for up to 4 hours. Serve from the top, removing the rounds as required.

BASKET-WEAVE WEDDING CAKE

This wonderful wedding cake can be made in any flavour. The butter icing design is really very easy and looks so special.

INGREDIENTS

Serves 150
- 1 × 25 cm/10 in, 1 × 20 cm/8 in and 1 × 15 cm/6 in square Madeira cakes
- 2.75 kg/6 lb/6 lb butter icing

DECORATION

- 1¹/₂ m/1¹/₂ yd × 2.5 cm/1 in wide pale lilac ribbon
- 2¹/₂ m/2¹/₂ yd × 5 mm/¹/₄ in wide deep lilac ribbon
- 30 fresh lilac-coloured freesias or simple flowers

MATERIALS AND EQUIPMENT

- 30 cm/12 in square silver cakeboard
- 20 cm/8 in thin silver cakeboard
- 15 cm/6 in thin silver cakeboard
- 12 greaseproof (wax) piping bags
- basket-weave and No. 4 plain writing nozzles

1 Make and bake the cakes one at a time, allow to cool, wrap in foil and store in a tin for up to one week before decorating.

2 If the cake tops have domed, cut a slice off to level the cakes, then invert the cakes onto their appropriate cakeboards. (It is quite a good idea to buy two larger thin cakeboards to sit the smaller cakes on while they are being decorated, to keep the edges neat. Allow an extra 2.5–5 cm/1–2 in.)

3 Make the butter icing in three batches. A food processor is worth using to obtain a very light texture and well mixed icing.

4 Spread each cake evenly with butter icing, dipping the palette knife (metal spatula) in hot water for easy spreading. Use a side scraper to smooth the sides and the palette knife to smooth the top. Leave in a cool place to set for at least one hour.

5 Make the remaining quantities of butter icing and make up at least 12 greaseproof (wax) paper piping bags. Fit a basket-weave nozzle in one bag and a No. 4 plain writing nozzle in a second greaseproof (wax) paper piping bag. Fill each with icing and fold down the tops.

6 Start piping the basket-weave design by piping a line of icing from the plain nozzle onto the corner of the large cake, from the base of the cake to the top. Using the basket-weave nozzle, pipe three horizontal lines across the vertical line, starting at the top of the cake and equally spacing the lines apart. Pipe another vertical line of icing on the edge of the

horizontal lines, then pipe three horizontal lines across this between the spaces formed by the previous horizontal lines to form a basket-weave. Pipe all around the side of the cake and neaten the top edge with a shell border, using the basket-weave nozzle. Repeat for the second cake.

7 To decorate the small cake with piping, pipe the top first by starting on the edge with one straight plain line, then pipe across with the basket-weave nozzle, spacing the lines equally apart, about the width of the nozzle. When the top is complete, carry on working the design around the sides, making sure the top and side designs meet. Leave all the cakes overnight in a cold place to set before assembling the cake.

8 Measure and fit the wide and narrow lilac ribbons around the board, securing with a pin. Use the remaining narrow ribbon to tie eight small bows with long tails. Select the flowers and trim off the stems.

9 To assemble the cake, carefully place the middle cake in position on the base cake, keeping it on the thin cakeboard the same size as the cake. Use a palette knife at the back of the cake to position it. Place the top cake on its board in position, using the palette knife at the back.

10 Position the bows on the top and base corners of the cakes. Place the flowers on each side of each cake at the corners of the board and a tiny arrangement on the top. This cake will keep all day in a cool place; if the weather is warm, position the flowers at the last minute to prevent wilting.

CHAMPAGNE WEDDING CAKE

An unusual combination of colours – champagne sugarpaste (fondant) and coffee-coloured ribbons and decorations – gives the cake an elegant, delicate appearance.

INGREDIENTS

Serves 120
- 1 × 25 cm/10 in, 1 × 20 cm/8 in and 1 × 15 cm/6 in round rich fruit cakes
- 120 ml/4 fl oz/1/2 cup apricot glaze
- 2.5 kg/5½ lb/5½ lb homemade or commercial white marzipan
- 3.25 kg/7 lb/7 lb champagne-coloured sugarpaste (fondant)
- 450 g/1 lb/1½ cups royal icing
- 575 g/1¼ lb/1¼ lb petal paste
- old gold and dark brown food colourings

DECORATION

- 5 m/5 yd × 2 cm/¾ in wide champagne ribbon
- 2 m/2 yd × 5 mm/¼ in wide champagne ribbon
- 4 m/4 yd × 1 cm/½ in wide coffee ribbon
- 2 m/2 yd × 5 mm/¼ in wide coffee ribbon
- 6 champagne-coloured cake pillars
- fresh cream or white flowers

MATERIALS AND EQUIPMENT

- 30 cm/12 in, 25 cm/10 in and 20 cm/8 in round silver cakeboards
- greaseproof (wax) paper piping bags
- No. 0 and 1 plain writing nozzles
- greaseproof (wax) paper
- crimping tool
- 5 acrylic cake skewers

1 Place each cake on its cakeboard and brush with apricot glaze. Cover each cake with marzipan.

2 Reserving 900 g/2 lb/2 lb of sugarpaste (fondant) for the cakeboards, use the remainder to smoothly cover each cake, starting with the largest cake. Leave in boxes overnight to dry in a warm, dry place. Knead all the sugarpaste (fondant) and trimmings together and cover the cakeboards. Replace the cakes on their boards and return to their boxes.

3 Make up the royal icing and the petal paste. Tint both icings with old gold food colouring to obtain the champagne colour of the sugarpaste (fondant) icing. Using a greaseproof (wax) paper piping bag fitted with a No. 1 plain writing nozzle, half-fill with royal icing. Measure and fit the wide champagne-coloured ribbon around each cakeboard, securing it with a pin.

4 To make the templates, measure and fit a band of greaseproof (wax) paper the same height around each cake. Fold the largest strip of paper into 6 equal sections, the next size into five sections and the small band into four sections. Place a plate on the edge of each template so that it comes halfway down the width. Draw around the shape and cut out.

5 Fit the appropriate template around each cake and mark the scalloped shape with an icing marker or pin. Remove the template. Fit the wide coffee-coloured ribbon around the base of each cake and secure with a bead of royal icing.

6 Knead the remaining sugarpaste (fondant) into the petal paste and, using a small piece at a time, make the frills one at a time (see Making Frills, overleaf). On the large cake pipe a line of icing following the design and apply the frill, pressing gently onto the cake. Once the first 6 frills have been fitted, apply the second layer of frills. Use a crimping tool to neaten the join. Repeat on each cake.

7 Pipe the bead and scroll design following the top edge of the frills and in-between the frills at the base. Colour some of the royal icing dark brown and over-pipe the design using a No. 0 plain writing nozzle. Tie 15 coffee-coloured bows and 15 champagne-coloured bows made from the fine ribbons and attach above and below the frills, where they join. Leave the cakes in their boxes to dry.

8 *Just before the wedding, place the cake pillars in position on the large and middle tier cakes. Press the skewers through the pillars into the cake. Mark the skewers level with the top of the pillars and carefully remove. Cut off the excess skewer above the pillars. Reassemble the cakes with the skewers and pillars, carefully placing each cake on top of the other. Decorate with a fresh flower arrangement on top of the cake and insert flowers in-between the pillars.*

91

The following templates have been reproduced at half actual size.

Large cake: template band folded into 6 equal sections.

Medium cake: template band folded into 5 equal sections.

Small cake: template band folded into 4 equal sections.

MAKING FRILLS

1 *Make one frill at a time, as follows. Roll out the paste thinly and cut out a round using a 7.5 cm/3 in plain or fluted cutter. Cut out the centre of the round using a 2.5 cm/1 in plain cutter. Alternatively, use a garrette frill cutter, as here.*

2 *Roll a cocktail stick or toothpick, sprinkled with cornflour (cornstarch), around the outer edge of the ring to frill. Cut the ring open with a sharp knife. Gently ease the frill open and attach to the cake, securing with royal icing.*

GOOD LUCK CAKE

This cake design would be ideal for a variety of occasions – a wedding, good luck, engagement or anniversary.

INGREDIENTS	DECORATION	MATERIALS AND EQUIPMENT
Serves 70	• *2 m/2 yd × 1 cm/¹⁄₂ in wide yellow ribbon*	• *28 cm/11 in round silver cakeboard*
• *25 cm/10 in horseshoe-shaped rich fruitcake (use quantities for a standard 20 cm/8 in round cake)*	• *2 m/2 yd × 2 cm/³⁄₄ in wide white ribbon*	• *V-shaped crimping tool*
• *45 ml/3 tbsp/3 tbsp apricot glaze*	• *2 m/2 yd × 2 mm/¹⁄₈ in wide yellow ribbon*	• *greaseproof (wax) paper*
• *900 g/2 lb/2 lb homemade or commercial white marzipan*		• *scalpel*
• *1.1 kg/2¹⁄₂ lb/2¹⁄₂ lb champagne-coloured sugarpaste (fondant) icing*		• *flower cutter*
• *300 g/11 oz/11 oz petal paste*		• *blossom plunger cutter*
• *yellow food colouring*		• *yellow stamens*
• *15 ml/1 tbsp/1 tbsp royal icing*		• *flower wire and tape*

1 Bake the cake and allow to cool. Brush with apricot glaze, place on the cakeboard and cover with marzipan.

2 Using about two-thirds of the sugarpaste (fondant), cover the cake smoothly. Knead all the sugarpaste (fondant) trimmings together and use to cover the cakeboard. Carefully remove the cake, then replace it after the board has been covered. Using a V-shaped crimping tool, crimp the top edge and base of the horseshoe cake. Do not crimp inside the base of the horseshoe, as it is difficult to fit the crimper into the space.

3 Cut a band of greaseproof (wax) paper the height of the cake to fit around the outside curve and over the ends of the horseshoe as a template. Measure and mark 1 cm/¹⁄₂ in intervals in the centre of the template (see Template, overleaf).

4 Fit the band around the cake, securing with two pins.

5 Cut through the marked lines with a scalpel to make slits the width of the wider yellow ribbon. Remove the template.

6 Insert the lengths of ribbons into alternate pairs of slits. Measure and fit the white and narrow yellow ribbon around the cakeboard and secure with a pin. Store the cake in a cake box in a warm, dry place until required.

7 Make up the petal paste, cut into three pieces and colour pale, medium and deep yellow. Make 31 cut-out flowers, using all the icing shades, and add stamens. Make 17 sprays of plunger blossoms using the stamens, flower wire and tape. Leave to dry overnight.

8 Arrange the sugar flowers on top of the cake and secure with a little royal icing. Place a few flowers on the cakeboard in-between the horseshoe and secure with royal icing.

This represents one-quarter of the complete template band; reproduced at actual size.

SWEETHEART CAKE

This romantic cake would be ideal for St Valentine's Day, or to celebrate an engagement or anniversary. Change the icing colours to suit the particular occasion.

INGREDIENTS

Serves 70
- 20 cm/8 in heart-shaped, light fruit cake (make using quantities for standard 23 cm/9 in round cake)
- 30 ml/2 tbsp/2 tbsp apricot glaze
- 900 g/2 lb/2 lb homemade or commercial white marzipan
- 900 g/2 lb/2 lb sugarpaste (fondant) icing
- red food colouring
- 225 g/8 oz/³/₄ cup royal icing

DECORATION

- 1 m/1 yd × 2.5 cm/1 in wide red ribbon
- 1 m/1 yd × 1 cm/¹/₂ in wide looped red ribbon
- ¹/₂ m/¹/₂ yd × 5 mm/¹/₄ in wide red ribbon
- fresh red rosebuds

MATERIALS AND EQUIPMENT

- 25 cm/10 in silver heart-shaped cakeboard
- large and medium-sized heart-shaped plunger cutters
- greaseproof (wax) paper piping bag
- medium star nozzle

1 Bake the cake and allow to cool. Brush with apricot glaze, place on the cakeboard and cover with marzipan. Using about three-quarters of the sugarpaste (fondant), cover the cake smoothly.

2 Trim away the excess sugarpaste (fondant). Knead the trimmings together with the remaining sugarpaste (fondant) and use to cover the cakeboard. Return the cake to the cakeboard and leave in a cake box to dry overnight.

3 Colour the remaining sugarpaste (fondant) bright red with red food colouring. Roll out thinly and cut out 18 large and 21 medium-sized hearts. Leave flat to dry.

4 Measure and fit the wide ribbon around the cakeboard and secure with a pin. Fit a band of the looped ribbon around the side of the cake, securing with a bead of icing. Tie a bow with long tails and attach to the side of the cake with a bead of icing.

5 Using a greaseproof (wax) paper piping bag fitted with a medium-sized star nozzle, fill with royal icing. Pipe a row of stars around the base of the cake and attach a medium-sized heart to alternate stars. Arrange the large red hearts around the top of the cake, and pipe a star to secure each one.

6 Choose several tiny rosebuds or one large rose and tie a bow with the remaining ribbons. Place on top of the cake just before serving.

GOLDEN WEDDING CAKE

For fifty years of marriage, you must have a special cake. With a fine lace edging, embossed horseshoes, bells and flowers, this anniversary cake will be exactly right.

INGREDIENTS

Serves 80
- 23 cm/9 in hexagonal rich fruit cake (make using quantities for a standard 23 cm/9 in round cake)
- 45 ml/3 tbsp/3 tbsp apricot glaze
- 1.1 kg/2½ lb/2½ lb homemade or commercial white marzipan
- 1.4 kg/3 lb/3 lb champagne-coloured sugarpaste (fondant) icing
- gold petal dust
- 300 g/11 oz/11 oz petal paste
- old gold food colouring
- 450 g/1 lb/1½ cups royal icing

DECORATION

- 1½ m/1½ yd × 2.5 cm/1 in wide gold ribbon
- 1½ m/1½ yd × 2 cm/¾ in wide gold ribbon
- 30 gold dragées
- '50' gold emblem
- 6 gold paper leaves

MATERIALS AND EQUIPMENT

- 28 cm/11 in hexagonal gold cakeboard
- horseshoe-shaped embossing tool
- bell mould
- foam sponge
- blossom plunger cutter
- flower stamens
- wire and tape
- sheet of perspex or glass
- run-out silk or greaseproof (wax) paper
- greaseproof (wax) paper piping bag
- No. 0 plain writing nozzle

1 Bake the cake and allow to cool. Brush with apricot glaze, place on the cakeboard and cover with marzipan. Using three-quarters of the sugarpaste (fondant), cover the cake smoothly.

2 Fit the wide ribbon around the base of the cake and secure with a pin. Measure and fit the narrower ribbon around the cakeboard, securing with a pin.

3 Using a horseshoe-shaped embossing tool and gold petal dust, emboss the sides of the cake with five horseshoes on each side and one on each corner. Place the cake in a box and leave in a warm place to dry.

Template design for lace pieces; reproduced at actual size.

4 Make up the petal paste and tint to a champagne colour using old gold food colouring. Using a well-cornfloured (cornstarched) bell mould, fill with a small piece of petal paste, pressing into the mould and rubbing the paste against the mould to make the shape. Trim the paste off at the edge and tap to release. Make three bells using two-thirds of the petal paste and leave to dry on a piece of foam sponge. Dust with gold petal dust when dry.

Reserve just a little petal paste. Using the remaining paste, blossom plunger and stamens, wire and tape, make up nine sprays of blossoms and leave to dry.

5 Make up the royal icing using double-strength egg albumen. Tint a champagne colour with old gold food colouring. Trace the lace design (see template) onto a sheet of paper and cover with a piece of perspex or glass. Cover this with a piece of run-out silk or greaseproof (wax) paper and secure with tape. Using a greaseproof (wax) paper piping bag fitted with a No. 0 plain writing nozzle, half-fill with icing. Follow the lace shapes, piping with fine threads of icing. Move the lace designs and continue to make 40 pieces, allowing for breakages.

CAKES FOR SPECIAL OCCASIONS

6 Attach the lace pieces to the top edge of the cake with a few beads of icing. Secure gold dragées in between, using icing to fix on. Press a small piece of petal paste into each bell shape and secure the sprays of blossoms just inside the bell openings. Arrange the bells in the centre of the cake, tilting the bells and supporting them on tiny pieces of petal paste.

7 Arrange the remaining ribbon in loops and secure in the centre of the bells, with the '50' emblem on top. Place the leaves in pairs in-between the bells and secure with royal icing. Leave to set.

SILVER WEDDING CAKE

This may look difficult, but it is really a simple cake to decorate once all the sugar pieces have been made.

INGREDIENTS

Serves 80
- 25 cm/10 in round rich or light fruit cake
- 60 ml/4 tbsp/4 tbsp apricot glaze
- 1.1 kg/2½ lb/2½ lb homemade or commercial white marzipan
- 1.4 kg/3 lb/4½ cups royal icing
- 575 g/1¼ lb/1¼ lb petal paste

DECORATION
- 50 large silver dragées
- 7 silver leaves
- '25' silver emblem
- 1½ m/1½ yd × 2.5 cm/1 in wide white ribbon
- 2 m/2 yd × 2.5 cm/1 in wide silver ribbon
- 1½ m/1½ yd × 5 mm/¼ in wide silver ribbon

MATERIALS AND EQUIPMENT
- 30 cm/12 in round silver cakeboard
- club cocktail cutter
- tiny round cutter
- greaseproof (wax) piping bag
- No. 1 plain writing nozzle

1 Bake the rich or light fruit cake and allow to cool. Brush with apricot glaze and cover with marzipan. Place the cake on the cakeboard.

2 Flat ice the top and sides of the cake with three or four smooth layers of royal icing. Leave to dry overnight, then ice the cakeboard. Place the cake in a box and dry in a warm, dry place. Reserve the remaining royal icing for decorations.

3 Measure and fit the white ribbon around the cakeboard and the wider silver ribbon around the sides of the cake; secure with a bead of icing.

4 Roll out small pieces of petal paste one at a time very thinly and, using a club cocktail cutter, cut out the sugar pieces. Using tiny round cutters, cut four holes out of each sugar piece. Make about 65 cut-out sugar pieces, allowing for breakages, and leave flat to dry overnight.

5 Arrange 25 cut-out pieces around the top of the cake so that they fit evenly. Using a greaseproof (wax) paper piping bag fitted with a No. 1 plain writing nozzle, half-fill with royal icing. Pipe small beads of icing onto the top edge of the cake and fit the sugar pieces in position. Repeat at the base of the cake, tilting the pieces upwards slightly. Pipe beads of icing in between each sugar piece and press a silver dragée in position. Leave the cake in a box to dry overnight.

6 Measure the finer silver ribbon to fit around the top edge of the sugar pieces, allowing enough to join. Very carefully thread the ribbon in and out of the sugar pieces, joining the ribbon at the back underneath the sugar pieces.

7 Arrange a circle of seven sugar pieces in the centre of the cake and secure each one with a bead of icing with seven silver dragées in between. Place the silver leaves and '25' emblem in position and secure with icing.

EASTER SPONGE CAKE

This light lemon quick-mix sponge cake is decorated with lemon butter icing and cut-out marzipan flowers.

INGREDIENTS

Serves 10–12
- 3-egg quantity lemon-flavoured quick-mix sponge cake
- 675 g/1½ lb/1½ lb lemon-flavoured butter icing
- 50 g/2 oz/½ cup flaked almonds, toasted
- 50 g/2 oz/2 oz homemade or commercial white marzipan
- green, orange and yellow food colouring

DECORATION

- 10 green cut-out marzipan flowers
- 8 orange cut-out marzipan flowers
- 6 cut-out marzipan daffodils

MATERIALS AND EQUIPMENT

- greaseproof (wax) paper
- 2 × 20 cm/8 in sandwich tins (shallow cake pans)
- nylon piping bag
- medium-sized gateau nozzle
- flower cutters

1 Preheat the oven to 160°C/325°F/Gas 3 and bake the cakes in two lined and greased 20 cm/8 in round sandwich tins (shallow cake pans) for 35–40 minutes until golden brown and the cakes spring back when lightly pressed in the centre. Loosen the edges of the cakes with a palette knife (metal spatula), turn out, remove the lining paper and cool on a wire rack.

2 Sandwich the cakes together with one-quarter of the butter icing. Spread the side of the cake evenly with another one-quarter of icing.

3 Press the almonds onto the sides to cover evenly. Spread the top of the cake evenly with another one-quarter of icing and finish with a palette knife (metal spatula) dipped in hot water, spreading backwards and forwards to give an even lined effect.

4 Place the remaining icing into a nylon piping bag fitted with a medium-sized gateau nozzle and pipe a scroll edging.

5 Using the marzipan and food colourings, make the cut-out marzipan flowers.

6 Arrange the marzipan flowers on the cake and leave the icing to set.

SIMNEL CAKE

This traditional Easter cake contains a layer of marzipan in the centre of a fruit cake mixture. A marzipan decoration also finishes the cake.

INGREDIENTS

Serves 10

- 450 g/1 lb/1 lb homemade or commercial white marzipan
- 225 g/8 oz/1½ cups raisins
- 175 g/6 oz/1 cup sultanas (golden raisins)
- 50 g/2 oz/⅓ cup glacé cherries, quartered
- 50 g/2 oz/⅓ cup cut mixed candied peel
- 175 g/6 oz/¾ cup butter, softened
- 175 g/6 oz/¾ cup caster (superfine) sugar
- 3 eggs
- 225 g/8 oz/2 cups plain (all-purpose) flour
- 5 ml/1 tsp/1 tsp baking powder
- 5 ml/1 tsp/1 tsp ground mixed spice
- 30 ml/2 tbsp/2 tbsp apricot glaze
- 1 egg, separated
- 175 g/6 oz/1 cup icing (confectioners) sugar, sifted

DECORATION

- 50 g/2 oz/2 oz homemade or commercial marzipan
- purple and green food colourings
- 3 purple marzipan cut-out flowers
- 11 green marzipan blossom flowers
- 1 m/1 yd × 2 cm/¾ in wide yellow ribbon
- 1½ m/1½ yd × 3 mm/⅛ in wide spotted yellow ribbon

MATERIALS AND EQUIPMENT

- 18 cm/7 in round deep cake tin
- flower cutter
- blossom plunger cutter

1 Cut the marzipan in half and roll out thinly on a surface lightly dusted with icing (confectioners) sugar. Using the base of an 18 cm/7 in round deep cake tin (pan), cut out the marzipan round.

2 Grease and double line the tin (pan) and preheat the oven to 170°C/325°F/Gas 3. Mix together in a bowl the raisins, sultanas (golden raisins), glacé cherries and mixed candied peel until evenly blended.

3 Place butter and sugar into a bowl, beat together until light and fluffy. Add in the eggs one at a time, beating well after each addition. Sift the flour, baking powder and mixed spice into the bowl and fold in gently, using a plastic spatula, until all the flour has been incorporated. Add the mixed fruit and fold in until evenly mixed.

4 Place half of the mixture in the tin (pan) and level. Place the marzipan round on top of the mixture, pressing down to level. Spoon the remaining cake mixture on top, smooth the top and make a slight depression in the centre. Bake in the oven for about 2¼–2½ hours until the cake is golden brown. Test with a skewer. Cool in the tin (pan), then turn the cake out, remove the paper and place on a wire rack.

5 Using two-thirds of the remaining marzipan, roll out and trim to an 18 cm/7 in circle. Brush the top of the cake with apricot glaze and cover with the marzipan round. Shape 11 small egg shapes, and form the remaining marzipan into a rope long enough to go around the top of the cake.

6 Secure the rope and eggs with apricot glaze.

7 Brush the marzipan evenly with egg yolk. Prepare a hot grill and sit the cake on a baking sheet. Grill (broil) the marzipan quickly until tinged with golden brown. Leave until cold.

8 Mix together the egg white and icing (confectioners) sugar and beat together until thick, glossy and white. Spread the icing in the centre of the cake and leave to set.

7

9 Using the marzipan and food colourings, make the flowers. Decorate the cake with flowers. Measure and fit the wide and spotted ribbons around the side of the cake. Tie a bow from the remaining spotted ribbon and secure the ribbons with a stainless steel pin.

CHOCOLATE FRUIT BIRTHDAY CAKE

A moist chocolate Madeira cake is covered in marzipan and chocolate fudge icing. The fruits are moulded from coloured marzipan and make an eye-catching decoration.

INGREDIENTS

Serves 30
- 18 cm/7 in square deep chocolate-flavoured Madeira cake
- 45 ml/3 tbsp/3 tbsp apricot glaze
- 450 g/1 lb/1 lb homemade or commercial white marzipan
- 450 g/1 lb/1 lb chocolate fudge icing
- red, yellow, orange, green and purple food colouring

DECORATION

- selection of marzipan fruits
- whole cloves
- angelica strips
- 0.75 m/¾ yd × 1 cm/½ in wide yellow ribbon

MATERIALS AND EQUIPMENT

- greaseproof (wax) paper
- 18 cm/7 in square deep cake tin (pan)
- 20 cm/8 in square silver cakeboard
- wire rack
- nylon piping bag
- medium-sized gateau nozzle

1 Bake the cake and allow to cool on a wire rack. Cut a slice off the top of the cake to level if necessary and invert on to the cakeboard. Brush evenly with apricot glaze.

2 Roll out two-thirds of the marzipan thinly to a 25 cm/10 in square. Place over the cake and smooth the top and down the sides. Trim off the excess marzipan around the base of the cake. Knead the trimmings together and reserve for making the marzipan fruits.

3 Place the cake on a wire rack over a tray and pour the freshly-made chocolate fudge icing over the cake, spreading quickly with a palette knife (metal spatula). Allow the excess icing to fall on the tray. Leave for 10 minutes, then place on to the cakeboard.

4 Using the remaining icing, place in a nylon piping bag fitted with a medium-sized gateau nozzle. Pipe a row of stars around the top edge and base of the cake. Leave to set.

5 Using the reserved marzipan, food colouring, cloves and angelica strips, model a selection of fruits.

6 Measure and fit the ribbon around the side of the cake and secure with a pin. Decorate the top with marzipan fruits.

EIGHTEENTH BIRTHDAY CAKE

A really striking cake for a lucky someone celebrating their eighteenth birthday. Change the shape if you cannot hire the tin (pan).

INGREDIENTS

Serves 80
- 33.5 × 20 cm/13½ × 8 in diamond-shaped deep rich or light fruit cake (make using quantities for a standard 23 cm/9 in round cake)
- 45 ml/3 tbsp/3 tbsp apricot glaze
- 1.1 kg/2½ lb/2½ lb homemade or commercial white marzipan
- 1.6 kg/3½ lb/3½ lbs white sugarpaste (fondant)
- black food colouring
- 30 ml/2 tbsp/2 tbsp royal icing

DECORATION

- 2 m/2 yd × 2.5 cm/1 in wide white ribbon
- ½ m/½ yd × 2 mm/⅛ in wide black ribbon

MATERIALS AND EQUIPMENT

- '18' numeral cutter or template
- greaseproof (wax) paper piping bag
- No. 1 plain writing nozzle

1 Bake the cake and allow to cool. Brush with apricot glaze and place on the cakeboard. Cover with marzipan.

2 Cover the cake using 1.1 kg/2½ lb/2½ lb sugarpaste (fondant). Knead the trimmings into the remaining sugarpaste (fondant) and colour using black food colouring.

3 Roll out two-thirds of the black sugarpaste (fondant) and cut into four strips the width and length of each section of the cakeboard. Brush the board with apricot glaze and place each strip in position; trim to fit neatly.

4 Roll-out one-quarter of the remaining sugarpaste (fondant) and cut out the number '18' using a special biscuit (cookie) cutter or by cutting round a template. Leave on a piece of foam sponge to dry.

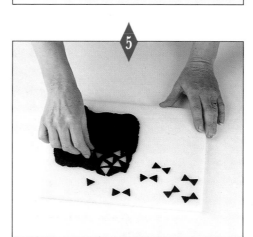

5 Roll out some more icing thinly and cut out 40 triangles for the bow ties and 20 for the wine glasses.

6 Use a tiny round cutter or the end of a plain nozzle to cut out 20 music notes and 10 bases for the glasses, cut in half. Cut out thin strips of icing for the tails of the music notes and the stems of the glasses.

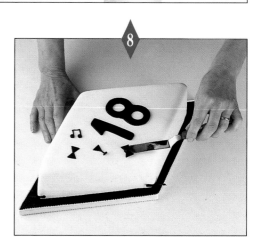

7 Using a greaseproof (wax) paper piping bag fitted with a No. 1 plain writing nozzle, half-fill with royal icing coloured black. Join the bow ties together with tiny beads of icing. Attach the music notes to their tails and the glasses to the stems and bases. Leave them all to dry.

8 Arrange the '18', music notes, wine glasses and bow ties over the top of the cake and attach each with a bead of icing. Continue to fix the decorations onto the sides of the cake.

TWENTY-FIRST BIRTHDAY CAKE

This cake looks good in any pale colour or simply white to suit the occasion. Add the colour with the ribbons and write your own personal message in the card.

INGREDIENTS

Serves 80
- 25 cm/10 in round rich fruit cake
- 45 ml/3 tbsp/3 tbsp apricot glaze
- 1.1 kg/2¹/₂ lb/2¹/₂ lb homemade or commercial white marzipan
- 1.4 kg/3 lb/4¹/₂ cups royal icing
- blue food colouring
- 575 g/1¹/₄ lb/1¹/₄ lb petal paste

DECORATION

- 1¹/₂ m/1¹/₂ yd × 2 cm/³/₄ in wide pale blue ribbon
- 1¹/₂ m/1¹/₂ yd × 1 cm/¹/₂ in wide royal blue ribbon
- 1¹/₄ m/1¹/₄ yd × 1.5 cm/⁵/₈ in wide looped royal blue ribbon
- 1¹/₄ m/1¹/₄ yd × 5 mm/¹/₄ in wide royal blue ribbon
- ³/₄ m/³/₄ yd × 2 mm/¹/₈ in wide royal blue ribbon

MATERIALS AND EQUIPMENT

- 30 cm/12 in round silver cakeboard
- 7.5 cm/3 in square fluted cutter
- 5 cm/2 in plain oval cutter
- No. 2 and 3 plain writing nozzle
- club-shaped cocktail cutter
- tiny petal cutter
- greaseproof (wax) paper piping bag
- blue food-colouring pen

1 Bake the cake and allow to cool. Brush with apricot glaze, cover with marzipan and place on a cakeboard.

2 Make the royal icing and colour pale blue with a few drops of blue food colouring. Flat-ice the top and sides of the cake with three layers of smooth royal icing. Leave the cake to dry, then ice the cakeboard. Reserve the remaining royal icing for decorating.

3 Make the petal paste and colour pale blue with a few drops of blue food colouring. Roll out about one-third of the paste thinly on a surface sprinkled with cornflour (cornstarch). Cut out two squares using the square fluted cutter. Cut out an oval shape from one square using the plain oval cutter. Make 2 tiny holes using a No. 2 plain writing nozzle on the left-hand edge, and match these on the plain square so that the ribbons will meet to tie the card together. Continue to make a cut-out pattern all around the card for the ribbon to thread through. Leave on a piece of foam sponge to dry.

4 Roll out some more petal paste thinly and, using a club-shaped cocktail cutter, cut out 25 shapes, allowing for breakage. Use a tiny petal cutter to cut out three shapes on each piece. Leave to dry.

5 To make the keys, roll out the paste thinly and cut two end shapes with the club cutter. Then, using a sharp knife, cut out two key shapes. Pattern the keys by using tiny cutters to make a pattern. Leave to dry.

6 Measure and fit the pale blue and royal blue plain ribbons around the board, securing with a pin. Fit the looped ribbon around the side of the cake and secure with a bead of icing.

7 Fit a greaseproof (wax) paper piping bag with a No. 3 plain writing nozzle and fill with blue icing. Arrange the 18 cut-out sugar pieces around the top edge of the cake and secure each with a bead of icing. Leave to dry. Pipe a shell edging around the base of the cake, and beads of icing in between the cut-out pieces around the top edge.

8 Using the food-colouring pen, write the message on the plain card and decorate the keys.

9 *Thread the ribbon through the matching holes to join the card together – do not tie too tightly or the card will not open – and tie a small bow with long ends.*

10 *Thread the remaining blue ribbon in and out of the cut-out sugar pieces on the top edge of the cake and join the ends together with a bead of icing underneath. Tie a bow and attach it to the side of the cake with a bead of icing. Arrange the card and key on top of the cake and place the remaining key on the cakeboard. Secure each with a little icing. Leave the cake to dry.*

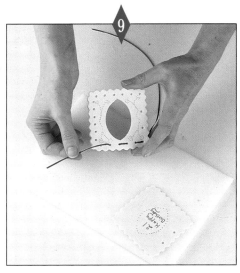

PETAL RETIREMENT CAKE

This cake is suitable for a special lady retiring from work. Choose any fresh flowers of your choice, such as lilies or freesias.

INGREDIENTS

Serves 50
- 20 cm/8 in petal-shaped deep light fruit cake (make using quantities for a standard 20 cm/8 in round cake)
- 45 ml/3 tbsp/3 tbsp apricot glaze
- 900 g/2 lb/2 lb homemade or commercial white marzipan
- 900 g/2 lb/2 lb sugarpaste (fondant) icing
- mulberry and pink food colouring
- 275 g/10 oz/10 oz petal paste
- 15 ml/1 tbsp/1 tbsp royal icing
- 1 egg white
- caster (superfine) sugar

DECORATION

- 2 m/2 yd × 2 cm/3/4 in wide white ribbon
- 2 m/2 yd × 1 cm/1/2 in wide fuchsia ribbon
- 2 m/2 yd × 2 mm/1/8 in wide fuchsia ribbon
- fresh flowers

MATERIALS AND EQUIPMENT

- 23 cm/9 in petal-shaped silver cakeboard
- foam sponge
- large and small blossom plunger cutters
- greaseproof (wax) paper piping bag
- No. 1 plain writing nozzle
- pink food colouring pen

1 Bake the cake and allow to cool. Brush with apricot glaze and place on the cakeboard. Cover the cake with marzipan.

2 Add some mulberry food colouring to the sugarpaste (fondant) and only knead lightly to give a marbled effect. Cover the cake with three-quarters of the sugarpaste (fondant) and leave to dry overnight. Roll out the remaining sugarpaste (fondant) and cover the cakeboard. Replace the cake in the centre of the board.

3 Make the petal paste and colour pink with food colouring. Roll out thinly and cut out an oblong 5 × 2.5 cm/2 × 1 in. Fold in half and dry over the end of a piece of foam sponge. Make four holes in the top edges of the fold to thread the ribbon through. Cut out 30 large and four small plunger blossom flowers and leave to dry.

4 Place the royal icing in a greaseproof (wax) paper piping bag fitted with a No. 1 plain writing nozzle. Measure and fit the white and fine fuchsia ribbon around the cakeboard, then the medium ribbon around the base of the cake. Secure all ribbons with beads of icing in the corner of the petal shapes. Tie six small bows from the fine ribbon and attach them to the base ribbon.

5 Attach the large blossom flowers around the side of the cake with beads of icing. Secure the remaining small blossom flowers to the card. Using the food colouring pen, write the message inside and draw a design. Thread some fine ribbon through the holes and tie a bow.

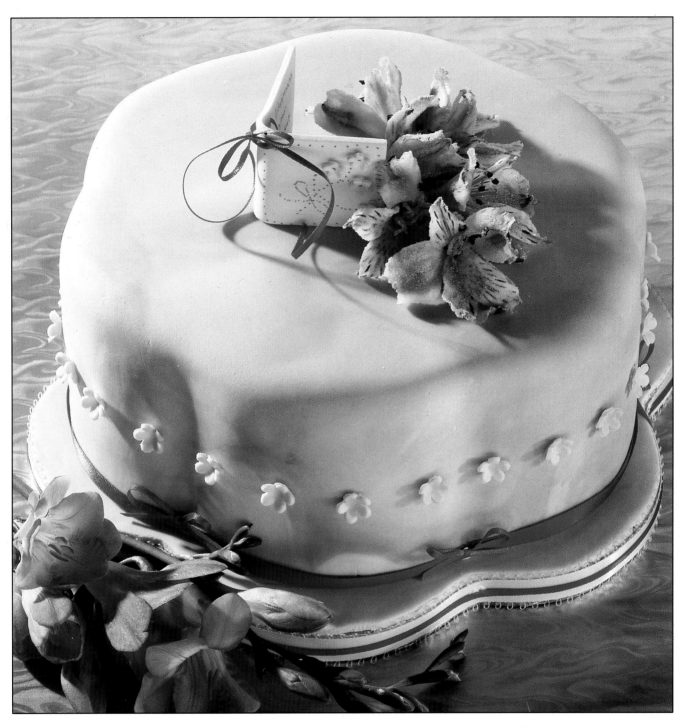

6 *Choose fresh flowers to match the ribbon on the cake, sugar-frost them with egg white and sugar and leave to dry. Arrange the flowers on the centre of the cake with the sugarpaste card.*

MOTHER'S DAY BASKET

Every mother would love to receive a cake like this on Mother's Day. Choose fresh flowers to decorate the top.

INGREDIENTS	DECORATION	MATERIALS AND EQUIPMENT
Serves 12 • 3-egg quantity of orange-flavoured quick-mix sponge cake • 900 g/2 lb/2 lb orange-flavoured butter icing	• 1 m/1 yd × 1 cm/½ in wide mauve ribbon • ½ m/½ yd × 2 mm/⅛ in wide spotted mauve ribbon • fresh flowers	• 1.1 l/2 pt/5 cup fluted ovenproof glass dish • 15 cm/6 in round silver cakecard • greaseproof (wax) paper piping bags • basket-weave nozzle • kitchen foil

1 Lightly grease and line the base of a fluted ovenproof glass dish (or brioche mould). Make the cake without any baking powder and bake in the oven for 1 hour 15 minutes to 1 hour 25 minutes until well risen, golden brown and firm to the touch.

2 Spread the side of the cake with one-third of the orange-flavoured butter icing and place upside down on a board.

3 Make plenty of greaseproof (wax) paper piping bags and fit with a basket-weave nozzle. Half-fill with butter icing and pipe the sides with a basket-weave pattern (see Basket-weave Wedding Cake).

4 Invert the cake onto the cakecard and spread the top with butter icing. Pipe a shell edging, using the basket-weave nozzle, to neaten the top edge. Continue to pipe the basket-weave icing across the top of the cake, starting at the edge. Leave the cake to set in a cool place.

5 Fold a piece of foil in half, then half again and continue to fold until you have a strip several layers thick.

6 Using the ribbon, bind the strip to cover the foil; bend up the end to secure the ribbon. Bend the foil to make a handle, and press into the icing.

7 Choose some flowers and make a neat arrangement tied with ribbon on top of the cake just before serving. Tie a bow and pin it to the sides of the cake.

FRILLS AND FLOWERS CHRISTENING CAKE

This pretty cake, decorated with flowers and frills, is perfect for a baby girl's Christening, and would be ideal for a little girl's birthday cake, too.

INGREDIENTS

Serves 50
- 20 cm/8 in round rich fruit cake
- 30 ml/2 tbsp/2 tbsp apricot glaze
- 800 g/1³/₄ lb/1³/₄ lb homemade or commercial white marzipan
- 1.1 kg/2¹/₂ lb/2¹/₂ lb sugarpaste (fondant) icing
- pink and red food colourings

DECORATION

- 2 m/2 yd × 1 cm/¹/₂ in wide deep pink ribbon
- 1¹/₂ m/1¹/₂ yd × 2 cm/³/₄ in wide deep pink ribbon
- 1 m/1 yd × 5 mm/¹/₄ in wide deep pink ribbon

MATERIALS AND EQUIPMENT

- 23 cm/9 in round silver cakeboard
- scalloped crimping tool
- greaseproof (wax) paper
- greaseproof (wax) paper piping bag
- No. 1 plain writing nozzle
- frill cutter
- large and medium blossom plunger cutters
- food-colouring pen

1 Bake the cake and allow to cool. Brush with apricot glaze, place on the cakeboard and cover the cake with marzipan. Tint the sugarpaste (fondant) pale pink using a few drops of pink food colouring. Using two-thirds of the sugarpaste (fondant), cover the cake. Fit the widest ribbon around the cakeboard and the narrowest ribbon around the base of the cake. Secure with a bead of icing.

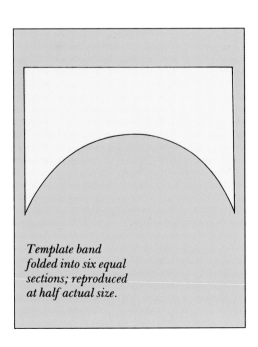

Template band folded into six equal sections; reproduced at half actual size.

2 Using a scalloped crimping tool, crimp the top edge of the cake by pressing the crimper into the icing but not squeezing it together.

3 Cut a strip of greaseproof (wax) paper to fit around the cake and of the same height. Fold the paper into six equal divisions and position a plate halfway over the template and draw around the shape. Cut out the shape to form the template and reserve the cut-out pieces. Fit the template around the cake and mark the shape with a scriber or pin. Remove the paper template.

4 Using a greaseproof (wax) paper piping bag fitted with a No. 1 plain writing nozzle, fill with royal icing. Using some of the remaining sugarpaste (fondant), roll and cut out a frill using a garrette frill cutter, but cut out a larger centre circle to make a thinner frill. Frill the edges (see Champagne Wedding Cake for general instructions). Make six frills, one at a time. Pipe a line of royal icing following the scalloped shape marked on the cake and attach the frill. Repeat to fit six frills.

5 Using a cut-out piece of the template, make a semi-circle shape to fit under the frill and mark ten 1 cm/¹/₂ in lines in a semi-circle for the ribbon insertion cuts. Transfer these marks to the side of the cake under each frill and cut the slits the same size as the ribbon. Cut the 1 cm/¹/₂ in wide ribbon into pieces to fit the gaps and insert five pieces under each frill.

6 Mark a 10 cm/4 in circle on top of the cake and mark 34 ribbon insertion lines. Cut the slits and insert 17 pieces of ribbon.

7 Knead all the sugarpaste (fondant) trimmings together and tint half dark pink to match the ribbon, using pink and red food colouring. Cut out 22 large and 40 medium light plunger blossom flowers, and 24 medium and 6 large dark plunger blossom flowers. Pipe a bead of icing in the centre of each.

8

9

8 Roll out a piece of dark pink sugarpaste (fondant) thinly and cut out a round using the frill cutter. Frill the edges, as above. Roll out the pale pink sugarpaste (fondant) and cut out a 5 cm/2 in fluted circle and place on top of the dark pink frill. Leave to dry. Attach eight plunger blossom flowers at the opposite sides of the plaque and secure with royal icing.

9 Using a food-colouring pen, dot in the design and write the child's name across the centre. Place in position on top of the cake. Mark the dark centres on the blossom flowers with the food-colouring pen. Attach the medium-sized dark pink flowers to the top edge of the cake and the large ones in the centre of the frilled scallop. Secure the medium light-pink flowers in-between the ribbon circle on top of the cake, and the small flowers on the side of the cake in-between the ribbon. Secure the remaining light pink flowers between each frill. Leave the cake to dry.

NOEL CHRISTMAS CAKE

For those who prefer a traditional royal-iced cake, this is a simple design using only one icing and easy-to-pipe decorations.

INGREDIENTS	DECORATION	MATERIALS AND EQUIPMENT
Serves 50	• 2½ m/2½ yd × 2 cm/¾ in wide gold ribbon	• greaseproof (wax) paper
• 20 cm/8 in round rich fruit cake	• 2½ m/2½ yd × 5 mm/¼ in wide red ribbon	• 23 cm/9 in round silver cakeboard
• 30 ml/2 tbsp/2 tbsp apricot glaze	• 44 large gold dragées	• greaseproof (wax) paper piping bag
• 800 g/1¾ lb/1¾ lb homemade or commercial white marzipan		• No. 1 and 2 × No. 0 plain writing nozzles
• 900 g/2 lb/3 cups royal icing		
• red and green food colouring		

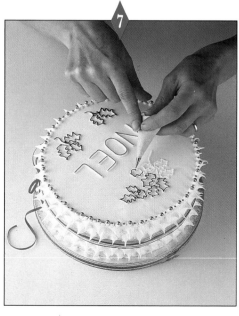

1 Bake the cake and allow to cool. Brush with apricot glaze, cover with marzipan and place on the cakeboard.

2 Flat-ice the top of the cake with two layers of royal icing and leave until dry. Ice the sides of the cake and peak the royal icing, leaving a space around the centre of the side to fit the ribbon. Reserve the remaining royal icing for decorating.

3 Pipe beads of icing around the top edge of the cake and attach a gold dragée on every other bead of icing.

4 Using a greaseproof (wax) paper piping bag fitted with a No. 1 plain writing nozzle, half-fill with royal icing. Write NOEL across the cake and then pipe holly leaves, stems and berries around the cake.

5 Measure and fit the gold ribbon around the side of the cake, taking care not to break the peaks. Press into the icing. Measure and fit the red ribbon over the top of the gold, and secure with a bead of icing. Tie a neat red bow and attach it to the front of the cake. Use the remaining ribbon to fit around the cakeboard, securing with a pin. Leave overnight to dry.

6 Colour 30 ml/2 tbsp/2 tbsp of the royal icing bright green and 15 ml/1 tbsp/1 tbsp bright red with food colouring paste. Use a greaseproof (wax) paper piping bag and a No. 0 plain writing nozzle. Over-pipe NOEL in red.

7 Pipe alternate dots around the edge of the cake in red for the berries and overpipe the holly in green. Leave to dry.

CHRISTMAS STOCKING CAKE

A bright and happy cake to make for Christmas. Make the stocking and parcels in advance to save time at Christmas.

Serves 50
- 20 cm/8 in square rich fruit cake
- 45 ml/3 tbsp/3 tbsp apricot glaze
- 900 g/2 lb/2 lb homemade or commercial white marzipan
- 1.1 kg/2½ lb/2½ lb sugarpaste (fondant) icing
- 15 ml/1 tbsp/1 tbsp royal icing
- red and green food colouring

DECORATION
- 1¼ m/1¼ yd × 2 cm/¾ in wide red ribbon
- 1 m/1 yd × 2 cm/¾ in wide green ribbon

MATERIALS AND EQUIPMENT
- 25 cm/10 in square silver cakeboard
- card for template

1 Bake the cake and allow to cool. Brush with apricot glaze and place on the cakeboard. Cover the cake with marzipan.

2 Reserve 225 g/8 oz/½ lb sugarpaste (fondant) icing for decorations, and use the remainder to cover the cake smoothly. Place the cake in a box and leave to dry in a warm dry place. Measure and fit the red ribbon around the board, securing with a pin, and the green ribbon around the cake, securing with royal icing.

Template for stocking; reproduced at half actual size.

3 Knead the sugarpaste (fondant) trimmings together. Reserve 125 g/4 oz/¼ lb and cut the remainder in half; colour one half red and the other half green with food colouring. Trace the template of the stocking onto card and cut out. Roll out a piece of white sugarpaste (fondant) and cut out round the template.

4 Roll out the red and green sugarpaste (fondant) to 5 mm/¼ in thick and cut each into seven 1 cm/½ in strips. Remove alternate green strips and replace with red strips. Gently roll the stripey sugarpaste (fondant) together.

5 Use the template to cut out another stocking shape, allowing an extra 5 mm/¼ in all around.

6 Brush the white stocking with apricot glaze and, using a palette knife (metal spatula), lift the striped stocking and place over the white one. Press lightly together and leave to dry.

7 Shape the remaining white sugarpaste (fondant) into four parcel shapes and trim each with thin strips of red and green sugarpaste (fondant) ribbons.

8 Knead the remaining green and red sugarpaste (fondant) together, keeping the colours separate. Roll out each into a 20 cm/8 in strip, 1 cm/½ in wide. Cut each into two 5 mm/¼ in strips. Pipe a bead of royal icing on to each corner, press alternate green and red strips in position and trim to size. Shape four red and four green balls and press in position where the sugarpaste (fondant) strips join, securing with a little royal icing.

9 Arrange the stocking and parcels in position on the top of the cake. Leave to dry.

MINI CHRISTMAS GIFT CAKES

These little cakes make a welcome gift, especially for friends or family on their own. Gift-wrap them in pretty boxes tied with ribbon.

INGREDIENTS

Makes 9
- 20 cm/8 in square rich fruit cake (make using quantities for a standard 18 cm/7 in round cake)
- 45 ml/3 tbsp/3 tbsp apricot glaze
- 675 g/1½ lb/1½ lb homemade or commercial white marzipan
- 450 g/1 lb/1 lb sugarpaste (fondant) icing
- 675 g/1½ lb/2¼ cups royal icing
- red, green and yellow food colouring

DECORATION

- 1 m/1 yd × 2 cm/¾ in wide green ribbon
- 1 m/1 yd × 5 mm/¼ in wide green ribbon
- 1 m/1 yd × 5 mm/¼ in wide red ribbon
- 1 m/1 yd × 2 cm/¾ in wide red ribbon
- 1 m/1 yd × 2 cm/¾ in wide gold ribbon
- 18 gold leaves
- 3 gold candles

MATERIALS AND EQUIPMENT

- 3 silver, 3 red and 3 gold 10 cm/4 in thin cakecards
- small crimping tool
- holly leaf cutter

1 Bake the cake and allow to cool. Cut the cake into three strips each way to make nine square cakes. Brush each with apricot glaze and place on a cakecard.

2 Cut the marzipan into nine pieces. Cut two-thirds off one piece and roll out a strip long enough and wide enough to cover the sides of one cake. Trim to size and wrap around the cake, keeping a good square shape. Roll out the remaining one-third of the marzipan large enough to fit the top. Invert the cake onto the square, trim to shape and replace on to the cakecard. Repeat to cover all the cakes with marzipan. Knead all the trimmings together and reserve for decorations.

3 Cut the sugarpaste (fondant) icing into three pieces. On a lightly sugared surface, roll out one piece at a time large enough to cover the top and sides of a cake. Cover the three cakes on the red cakecards. Crimp the top edges of each cake using a small crimping tool.

4 Cover the three cakes on the gold cards with royal icing and peak the surfaces to finish, working on one cake at a time. Leave a strip plain around the sides to fit the ribbons.

5 Cut the marzipan trimmings into three portions. Colour one red, one green and the other piece yellow. Roll out the green marzipan thinly and cut out 27 leaves, using a holly leaf cutter. Mark the veins with a knife and bend the leaves. Make lots of tiny red berries, and form the remaining red marzipan into nine candle shapes – three small, three medium and three large. Shape nine flames from the yellow marzipan. Arrange the candles, flames, holly leaves and berries on the sugarpaste cakes and tie each with a wide red ribbon and a bow. Secure all the decorations with a little royal icing.

6 *Arrange a holly garland on the plain marzipan cakes with a few berries. Tie each marzipan cake with wide green and fine red and green ribbon and a double bow.*

7 *Arrange the six gold leaves on each peaked royal icing cake. Position a gold candle in the centre and the gold ribbon around each cake with a bow. Leave all the cakes to set overnight before gift-wrapping them.*

MARZIPAN BELL CAKE

An unusual Christmas cake, this is decorated purely with marzipan which gives a Christmas feel without the sweetness of icing.

INGREDIENTS	DECORATION	MATERIALS AND EQUIPMENT
Serves 40	• 1 m/1 yd × 2 cm/³/4 in wide red ribbon	• 20 cm/8 in round silver cakeboard
• 18 cm/7 in round rich or light fruit cake	• 1 m/1 yd × 5 mm/¹/4 in wide green ribbon	• crimping tool
• 30 ml/2 tbsp/2 tbsp apricot glaze	• ¹/4 m/¹/4 yd × 5 mm/¹/4 in wide red ribbon	• bell cutter
• 900 g/2 lb/2 lb homemade or commercial white marzipan		• holly leaf cutter
• green, yellow and red food colouring		

1 Bake the cake and allow to cool. Brush with apricot glaze and place on the cakeboard.

2 Colour two-thirds of the marzipan pale green with a few drops of green food colouring. Knead until evenly coloured.

3 Roll out the marzipan to a 23 cm/9 in circle and place over the cake, smoothing across the top and down the side. Trim the excess marzipan away from the base of the cake. Using a crimping tool, crimp the top edge of the cake to make a scalloped pattern.

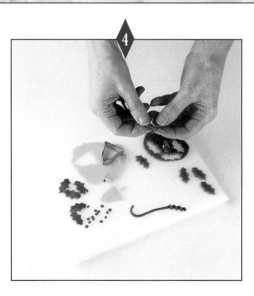

4 Colour a small piece of marzipan bright yellow, a small piece bright red and the remaining trimmings and marzipan bright green.
　Roll out the yellow marzipan and using a bell cutter, cut out two bells and mould two clappers.
　Using some green marzipan, cut two pencil-thin lengths and form into bell ropes, bending them into shape. Roll out the remaining green marzipan and using a holly cutter, cut out eleven holly leaves. Mark the veins with a knife and bend them to shape.
　Using the red marzipan, shape some tiny red berries and also two thin strips to wind around the end of the bell ropes. Leave the decorations to dry.

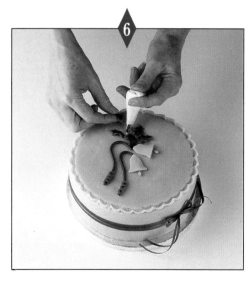

5 Measure and fit the wide red and fine green ribbon around the side of the cake, securing each with a pin. Tie a neat double bow from red and green fine ribbon and attach to the side with a bead of icing.

6 Arrange the bells, clappers, bell ropes, holly leaves and berries on top of the cake and secure each with a little apricot glaze.

USEFUL SUPPLIERS AND ADDRESSES

Great Britain

THE BRITISH SUGARCRAFT GUILD
Wellington House, Messeter Place, Eltham, London SE9 5DP.

CAKE ART LTD
Wholesale suppliers of icings and equipment. Unit 16, Crown Close, Crown Industrial Estate, Priors Wood, Taunton, Somerset TA2 8RX.

SUGARCRAFT SUPPLIERS PME (HARROW) LTD
Suppliers of decorating equipment. Brember Road, South Harrow, Middlesex HA2 8UN.

JF RENSHAW LTD
Suppliers of icings. Locks Lane, Mitcham, Surrey CR4 2XG.

ESSEX ICING CENTRE
Suppliers of materials and equipment. 20 Western Road, Billericay, Essex CM12 9DZ.

INVICTA BAKEWARE LTD
Manufacturers and suppliers of bakery equipment. Westgate Business Park, Westgate Carr Road, Pickering, North Yorkshire YO18 8LX.

CRANHAM CATERING
Suppliers of materials and equipment. 95 Front Lane, Cranham, Upminster, Essex RM14 1XN.

CRAIGMILLAR
Suppliers of icings. Stadium Road, Bromborough, Wirral, Merseyside LO2 3NU.

PROMODEM LTD
Technical consultancy and suppliers of cake tilters. 141 Grange Road, Great Burstead, Billericay, Essex CM11 2SA.

SQUIRES KITCHEN
Squire House, 3 Waverley Lane, Farnham, Surrey GU9 8BB.

E RUSSUM & SONS
Edward House, Tenter Street, Rotherham.

THE HOUSE OF SUGARCRAFT
Suppliers of flower cutters, powder and paste colours and piping tubes. Unit 10, Broxhead Industrial Estate, Lindford Road, Bordon, Hampshire GU35 0NY.

CEL CAKES
Suppliers of modelling tools, containers and display cabinets. Springfield House, Gate Helmsley, York, North Yorkshire YO4 1NF.

JENNY CAMPBELL TRADING/B R MATTHEWS AND SON
12 Gypsy Hill, Upper Norwood, London SE19 1NN.

CYNTHIA VENN
3 Anker Lane, Stubbington, Fareham, Hampshire PO14 3HF.

KNIGHTSBRIDGE BUSINESS CENTRE (WILTON UK)
Knightsbridge, Cheltenham, Gloucestershire GL51 9TA.

RAINBOW RIBBONS
Unit D5, Romford Seedbed Centre, Davidson Way, Romford, Essex RM7 0AZ.

South Africa

SOUTH AFRICAN SUGARCRAFT GUILD
National Office, 1 Tuzla Mews, 187 Smit Street, Fairlan 2195.

JEM CUTTERS
PO Box 115, Kloof, 3 Nisbett Road, Pinetown 3600.

North America

ICES (INTERNATIONAL CAKE EXPLORATION SOCIETY)
Membership enquiries: 3087–30th St. S.W., Ste.101, Grandville, MI 49418.

MAID OF SCANDINAVIA
Equipment, supplies, courses, magazine Mailbox News. *3244 Raleigh Avenue, Minneapolis, MN 55416.*

WILTON ENTERPRISES INC
2240 West 75th Street, Woodridge, Illinois 60517.

HOME CAKE ARTISTRY INC
1002 North Central, Suite 511, Richardson, Texas 75080.

LORRAINE'S INC
148 Broadway, Hanover, MA 02339.

CREATIVE TOOLS LTD
3 Tannery Court, Richmond Hill, Ontario, Canada L4C 7V5.

MCCALL'S SCHOOL OF CAKE DECORATING INC
3810 Bloor Street, Islington, Ontario, Canada M9B 6C2.

Australia

AUSTRALIAN NATIONAL CAKE DECORATORS' ASSOCIATION
PO Box 321, Plympton, SA 5038.

CAKE DECORATING ASSOCIATION OF VICTORIA
President, Shirley Vaas, 4 Northcote Road, Ocean Grove, Victoria 3226.

CAKE DECORATING GUILD OF NEW SOUTH WALES
President, Fay Gardiner, 4 Horsley Cres, Melba, Act, 2615.

CAKE DECORATING ASSOCIATION OF TASMANIA
Secretary, Jenny Davis, 29 Honolulu Street, Midway Point, Tasmania 7171.

CAKE DECORATORS' ASSOCIATION OF SOUTH AUSTRALIA
Secretary, Lorraine Joliffe, Pindari, 12 Sussex Crescent, Morphet Vale, SA 5162.

CAKE ORNAMENT CO
156 Alfred Street, Fortitude Valley, Brisbane 4006.

New Zealand

NEW ZEALAND CAKE DECORATORS' GUILD
Secretary, Morag Scott, 17 Ranui Terrace, Tawa, Wellington.

DECOR CAKES
RSA Arcade, 435 Great South Road, Otahaha.

INDEX

ACKNOWLEDGEMENTS

Janice Murfitt would like to thank the following: Mavis Giles for her unfailing ability to type illegible copy at a minute's notice; Jean Ainger for supplying equipment and sugarcraft props for photography; Cake Fayre, 11 Saddlers Walk, 44 East Street, Chichester, W Sussex, PO19 1HQ (Tel. 0243 771857).